# CONTENTS

CHRISTOPHER MEEHAN

# pursued
# *by*
# GOD

---

*The Amazing Life and*

*Lasting Influence of*

# JOHN
# CALVIN

FAITH
ALIVE
Christian Resources

Grand Rapids, Michigan

We welcome your comments. Call us at 1-800-333-8300, or e-mail us at editors @faithaliveresources.org.

**Library of Congress Cataloging-in-Publication Data**
Meehan, Christopher H., 1949-
Pursued by God : the amazing life and lasting influence of John Calvin / Christopher Meehan.
    p. cm.
Includes bibliographical references.
ISBN 978-1-59255-503-1
1. Calvin, Jean, 1509-1564. 2. Calvin, Jean, 1509-1564—Influence. I. Title.
BX9418.M37 2009
284'.2092—dc22
[B]

2009017193

160610

10 9 8 7 6 5 4 3 2 1

# PREFACE

---

I t may seem strange that a Catholic boy like me would end up researching and writing a book about John Calvin, but it is my hope that seeing Calvin through these eyes might offer a fresh look at this vitally important figure in the history of the church.

It's not as though I come to Calvin with no understanding of the man and his legacy at all. For many years I have worked as a newspaper and magazine journalist in Grand Rapids, Michigan, where Calvinist churches and educational institutions dot the landscape. And I now work in the communications department of the Christian Reformed Church.

In my own study of Calvin, I sensed the hold that the Catholic Church had on him, for good and for ill, starting from his youth. The man we honor in 2009 on the occasion of his five hundredth birthday did not hate the Catholic Church. Brought up within its often warm embrace, Calvin portrayed himself as a person who was simply trying to bring that church back to the truth of the gospel.

He wanted to rid the church of its superstitions, indulgences, and its overemphasis on saints and Mary, Christ's mother, to whom people prayed at the expense of the centrality of Jesus Christ. Even more, he wanted to rescue the profound beauty and meaning of the sacraments from the encrusted rituals and almost magical interpretations that had emerged in medieval Catholicism. The church, Calvin believed and taught and wrote, had to focus first and always on Jesus and his teachings, and on the reality that Christ was God who lived among his people in the flesh. Along with reformers such as Martin Luther, Calvin worked hard to bring the focus of the church back to where he believed it should be.

Strangely, in writing about Calvin my own faith was renewed. I experienced a deeper appreciation for the centrality of Jesus. As an active Catholic working for a Reformed organization, I began to see that at heart we believe many of the same things, although important doctrines, or, in some cases, simply assessments of them, still divide us. In writing this book I tried keep the focus on the unity Calvin worked for—one church worshiping the one God.

Of course, there is much more to Calvin than just his Catholic heritage and his work toward unifying the church. He was a writer, thinker, teacher, and preacher who offered the world new ways of looking at things and new ways of thinking about things, and, as a consequence, new ways of living. In his vast writings Calvin left an important legacy often called "Calvinism" or "the Reformed tradition." This legacy—which consists of a richness of ideas on subjects as varied as the depths of human sinfulness and the wide range of human possibilities in God's creation—is alive and well today in many churches, and not all of them of the Reformed variety, around the world.

Above all, I was moved by Calvin's vital faith, his devotion to doing God's will, and his willingness to offer his life for the service of Christ's Church. Parts of his personality were rough-edged—the word *irascible* comes to mind. He spoke his mind with blunt eloquence. But he wasn't the Protestant pope, the dictator of Geneva, the heartless instigator of witch hunts and heresy trials. He was a man of his age, and at the same time his ideas transcended his time to be rediscovered and widely recognized today.

I also discovered in Calvin a man who was a fearless ambassador for Christ, a faithful pastor, and a loving husband, stepfather, and brother.

Ultimately I came to see him as a gifted and passionate Christian brother who was captured by the one who rose from the dead on that first glorious Easter morning.

*Easter 2009*

# Chapter 1

# IN THE SHADOW
# OF THE CATHEDRAL

---

Nestled atop a hill, the twin towers of the Roman Catholic Cathedral seemed to soar high into the sky above the modest home in which John Calvin grew up. It was by far the tallest—and the oldest—structure in the town of Noyon, France. Doubtless the young Calvin darted in and out among its long shadows spreading across the town square as he played with his friends or ran off on some errand for his parents. Erected in 1131 in the traditional shape of a Latin cross, this solemn and foreboding structure had a fascinating and even gruesome history. Most of the bishops who had served there over the centuries were entombed inside, and many were represented by statues that stood like sentinels before their crypts. It must have seemed awesome and a little frightening to the boy.

A good Catholic boy, John Calvin attended many services inside the massive stone sanctuary filled with religious paintings and a plethora of side altars. He walked its dim hallways and listened to the echoes. His parents taught Calvin that Jesus Christ lived inside the church in the form of the bread and wine that were given special places of honor at the front; these were no mere symbols. Young Calvin prayed there, attended Mass, made his confession to the priest. Walking along its flying buttresses, he would hear its five bells tolling the hours. Catholicism as embodied in the Cathédrale Notre-Dame in Noyon was an anchor in the boy's early life.

It may seem a bit odd that traditional Catholicism played such an integral role in the youth of the man we know now as a great Protestant reformer. Yet this was the powerful and pervasive institution that he dedicated many years of his life to reform. His intimate knowledge of its intricate web of power, law, and doctrine proved enormously helpful in later years when he found himself confronting its monolithic authority.

## A BOY FROM NOYON

From his early years, it was clear that young Calvin was very precocious. Early on, according to one biographer, he "displayed both the intellectual and personal qualities which were destined to lay their stamp on his life work." Evidently Calvin had a capacity from a very young age to learn and to retain what he was taught. But there were many smart boys in the town by the Oise River. What no one could guess was that God had great plans for this child. As a young man, Calvin would construct a cathedral of ideas that would not only shake the world of his day but would deeply influence the institutions and thinking of twenty-first century North Americans.

By forsaking the church of his forebears, Calvin would form a new branch of Christ's church that took root and spread around the world for centuries to come. This young man, certainly with the help of other reformers, shaped a faith tradition that would serve as a guidepost for a clear-eyed, compassionate, and disciplined approach to life and worship for millions of people of many ethnic groups and races. In fact, the message and theology of John Calvin have as much relevance today in 2009—the year that we celebrate his five hundredth birthday—as they did at the start of the Reformation. Calvin spent his life articulating a faith that remained strong over the centuries and that seems to be enjoying a rebirth in the tumultuous early years of the twenty-first century. As John Calvin would readily admit, his is a story of God's leading. But it is also an amazing tale about a young boy from Noyon. It is the story of a young man who could not find what his heart and mind most deeply craved in the Catholic Church, and who dramatically turned elsewhere to find it. It is the story of a mature and gifted reformer whose deep faith, prophetic voice, keen mind, and sometimes harsh words challenged the world of his day.

Our knowledge of Calvin's early life is somewhat thin, but here are some of the things we know for sure. He was born Jean Cauvin on July 10, 1509, in Noyon, France. Small as it was, the town had an illustrious history. The great Charlemagne was crowned king of the Franks there in 768. We also know that this town, located in the Picardy region and situated on a road built by the Romans, never had much industry. The rich, loamy farmland sustained a thriving agricultural countryside. In fact, Calvin's home was right across the street from the corn market, the place to which outlying farmers brought their goods to market. With the market nearby and the cathedral around the corner, Calvin lived in the bustling center of the town.

The streets and alleys of Noyon, its homes and churches, its people and businesses, were etched in Calvin's mind. As a young boy, he often made forays from his home, enchanted and sometimes disturbed by all that he saw—the drunks, the happy couples, the tired workers, the clergy, the ragtag groups of rough-looking teens, the old buildings, the forest beyond town, and, of course, the looming towers of the cathedral. Long after leaving, he continued to write people still living there, catching up on the news. He frequently referred to Noyon with a sense of nostalgia in his later correspondence. One biographer tells us Calvin was deeply disturbed when the Spaniards nearly destroyed the town while he was a preacher in Geneva. He experienced a special sense of anger and loss since the Spaniards had also done this in his childhood just before he went off to college. Word of the pillaging brought back bad memories and led him to pray for the safety of the people left in Noyon, some of whom were still good friends of his.

## EARLY INFLUENCES

If you weren't a farmer, your best bet for making a decent livelihood in Noyon was getting on the payroll of the church. It was the center of official Catholicism in that part of France, the seat of the Bishopric of Noyon. Young Calvin could smell the incense and hear the ringing of bells to signal the start of Mass. He was familiar with the Latin prayers on everyone's lips, whether they knew the language or not. The Roman faith saturated the very atmosphere. Women were always praying the rosary, counting off the beads, reciting "Hail Marys" as they nursed their children, sold produce, or simply stood on their small porches, watching the late medieval world of northern France unfold.

John Calvin's father, Gérard, was one of those who worked for the church. An ambitious man, a lawyer by trade, he held many titles. Essentially he served as a chief financial officer for the bishop who lived in that town. The bishop ruled the church life and, to an extent, the secular life of the surrounding area. Gérard grew up in a working-class family of dock workers and coopers, tradesmen who fixed barrels, in the fishing village of Pont-l'Evêque near Normandy, not far north of Noyon. But even from his youth, we suspect that Gérard was bored by the slow movement of small-town life. He craved the intense activity of a larger place. He itched to move somewhere else, to become someone of substance. So he worked hard to enter a profession.

Gérard came to Noyon in 1481, and by 1497 his leadership skills and ambition had made him a minor member of the ruling class. He had become friends with the powerful deHangest family, from which came two bishops who served the Catholic Church during Gérard Calvin's time. Over the years, Gérard's official duties took him from being a simple registrar employed by the government of Noyon on up through the ranks. He ultimately became an agent for the county, attorney for the clergy connected to the cathedral, and finally secretary to the bishop.

All this left Gérard with little time for a social life. But at forty he married the beautiful and devout Jeanne Le Franc, daughter of an innkeeper and city council member from the nearby town of Cambrai, a community of some significance and power in that part of France. Likely his new bride brought with her a dowry that helped to boost Gérard's resources. We know that she taught her son John to pray, giving him a sense of God's majesty, power, and love. Jeanne was a strong Catholic who never veered from her faith. Had she lived, she would have been astonished to realize what her little boy would accomplish.

Gérard Calvin doesn't seem to have shared her devotion, but he did earn a decent income—at least enough to support Jeanne and then a second wife when the innkeeper's prayerful daughter died only a few years after they married. In all, Gérard had five sons and two stepdaughters. John, the second son, was baptized soon after his birth at a nearby parish church. His mother died when he was about five.

Charles, the oldest brother, grew up to serve for a time as a priest. Apparently, though, he had a fiery personality, and was branded a heretic for punching another priest, among other things. Ultimately he was excommunicated from the church and executed. But that came much later—after Gérard had his own troubles with church authorities.

Another brother, Antoine, was close to John for most of his life and accompanied him on many of his travels. Although we don't know much about Antoine, we do know of a saucy story that entangled both of them. Once John and his brother had settled for good in Geneva, Antoine married a woman who ended up leaving him for a handsome hunchback. Having his beloved brother cuckolded under the roof of the home they shared would cause John, by then a famous preacher and reformer, untold grief. John had to appear before civil authorities in Geneva to plead Antoine's case, and he was able to win his brother a divorce. Of the fourth brother, Francois, little is known, other than he died at a young age. Another son, also named Antoine, died young as well.

By all accounts, Gérard worked hard to serve the interests of the bishop. But we know that Gérard had a furious temper, a troublesome attribute he apparently handed down to John, and, of course, his oldest son Charles. Some writers tell us that John Calvin's father would occasionally denounce the canons, the men who held various offices and duties of the church for which he worked. He'd get so angry at what he saw as the duplicity and hypocrisy of the clergy that he would raise his voice, shouting and stalking around until his wife calmed him down.

Strangely, in his own voluminous writings, Calvin rarely mentions his father, and when he does it is with little emotion. Gérard's entire focus seemed to be on his work and the intrigues of the church. John respected and obeyed his father, but it's unlikely they enjoyed a close or loving relationship. Maybe they were too much alike to get along: both had probing minds and sensitive but reclusive natures. Back then, there was no strong tradition of intimate, lasting relationships between fathers and sons. In fact, it is quite probable that Calvin received a harsh whipping or two from his father when he got out of line. At the same time, it is hard to imagine young John causing too much trouble, since he seems to have stayed above the fray and held his own counsel even as a youth. In any case, Gérard recognized John's intellectual potential and sent him away to school as a young teen. After that John never came home to stay. If they corresponded, no letters remain to better define their relationship.

So what influences, besides John Calvin's distant father and his short-lived though prayerful mother, could have helped shape the future reformer?

*Chapter 2*

# WINDS OF CHANGE

---

C alvin's early influences extended beyond his family and his education. Some historians believe that the countryside and culture in which he grew up also shaped him. Picardy was a land of castles and cathedrals, lakes and rivers, forests, farm fields, marshes, and, near the northern Normandy coast, even sand dunes. The area was widely recognized for producing young men who were tough and often fiercely controversial. But these young men also had the reputation for being sensitive, proud, forthright, and logical. While geography doesn't explain everything, Calvin had all of those traits. It would be hard to argue that the Picardy in his blood didn't, to some extent, help make him who he was.

Another influence on Calvin, of course, was the times themselves. During this period, Europe was moving out of the Middles Ages into the Renaissance—a time of explosion in humanistic literature, art, and thought. In addition, the Reformation movement had already begun in Germany, England, and Eastern Europe. Known for its chaos as well as its flood of new ideas, this was a period of enormous change. Columbus had just discovered a new world; the Turks were on the advance in the Middle East; music was breaking out of old forms; art and architecture were flowering. Scientists and explorers were raising new questions about the place of humanity on this planet. It was the era of Copernicus, who proved that earth moved around the sun; Pizzaro, who conquered the Incan Empire; Michelangelo, who painted the Sistine Chapel; Shakespeare, who penned astounding plays and poetry; and Magellan, who circled the globe in a ship.

Much of this change occurred well outside Calvin's life in Noyon. But in years to come the events and personalities and passionate ideas of his day sparked his imagination and challenged his questioning mind. Eventually he would become one of the most sought-after thinkers, preachers, and writers of his age.

Above all, the young Calvin was immersed in the Catholic world of Noyon, whose cathedral bells clocked his hours and defined his days. During his youth he seemed to have no problems with this; more likely he appreciated and loved aspects of this life that centered on God.

Still, the church for which Calvin's father worked, and whose life pervaded every corner of Noyon, was starting at this very time to come under assault from such firebrands as Martin Luther in Germany and Ulrich Zwingli in Switzerland. Both men based their beliefs on the Bible and on books of theology and philosophy that had become widely available after the invention of the printing press only a few decades before. Both strongly opposed the Vatican's sale of indulgences to help fund construction of Saint Peter's Basilica in Rome. Indulgences came from performing certain acts of charity, from praying certain prayers, and from paying money to the clergy. These indulgences were supposedly to help God-fearing people spend less time in purgatory and speed their transition into heaven. They were a great moneymaker for the pope in Rome.

By the time Calvin was growing up, the Reformation in Germany and Switzerland had started to influence people in France as well. In France, scholars say, the Reformation took on a humanist quality, somewhat different from the more dogmatic style of Germany and Switzerland. Humanism was a movement that emphasized the literature and culture of antiquity from recently rediscovered books. Humanists revered classical literature and considered the narrow rigors of scholastic thinkers such as Thomas Aquinas inferior. They considered it their task to retrieve the wisdom and beauty of the past and bring them to bear on life and religion in their own day.

One of the most famous humanists was a Roman Catholic theologian named Desiderius Erasmus. In 1516 he published an annotated edition of the Greek New Testament that included a Latin translation. In 1519 he also published a multivolume work on St. Jerome, the patron saint of librarians and one of the most learned of the Fathers of the early church. In both of these, Erasmus offered a more rational conception of Christian doctrine, hoping to open people's minds and lift them from the rigid theology of more recent times. Erasmus eventually became one of John Calvin's humanist heroes.

## A PATH TOWARD ORDINATION

Thus the slow rumble of a theological upheaval began to be heard outside of Noyon. This had little impact on the young John Calvin, who had been placed on a path to ordination as a priest. When he was twelve years old, he underwent a ceremony in which the bishop snipped his hair into a tonsure, setting him on the road toward full-fledged priesthood and then into the bureaucracy of the church. The sacred rite of the tonsure, although not necessarily limited to those who were well-off, was normally given to those in good financial or social circumstances.

It's safe to assume Calvin received the tonsure with pride, and that his father's influence with the bishop helped to bring it about. This ceremony, in effect, made him an unofficial part of the clergy. Tonsured young men were usually assigned to work under priests in various chapels, often in roles that were more of a figurehead, while ordained priests did the real work. Calvin was eventually placed in such a position at the church of St. Martin de Marteville. He later found a position as pastor in his father's home village of Pont-l'Evêque. These appointments put him in line to receive generous stipends to pay for his schooling. Calvin, however, did a little preaching in some of the churches to which he had been named chaplain, a role he came to relish. He may also have done some preaching as a small way of paying back the stipends he was given to go to college. Calvin seemed to be happy with this arrangement. His father, Gérard, wanted him to be a priest, and he willingly followed this path.

Surrounded by all the trappings of the church, young Calvin was not critical of the Roman Catholic Church during the time of his tonsure. Exactly how deeply he experienced and practiced his faith is not recorded. But evidently he embraced the church early on. When he was very young, his mother had him light candles and pray regularly to the saints and to Mary, the mother of Jesus. Once she took her little boy on a pilgrimage to the nearby valley of the shrine of St. Anne, the mother of Mary and the earthly grandmother of Jesus. "Lifted by his pious mother," says one biographer, "young John kissed the precious relic of the skull of St. Anne as it lay on its golden receptacle, surrounded by candles and flowers and the adoring faces of other pilgrims."

Calvin himself recollected observing many feasts and celebrations tied to the church's liturgy. Writing with a critical eye many years later, he recalls "seeing as a little boy what was happening to images in our parish church. On the feast of St. Stephen, December 26, people decorated with chaplets and ribbons not only the image of the saint himself, but also those of the tyrants (to give them a common name) who stoned him. When the credulous women saw tyrants dressed up like this, they took them for companions of the saint and burned a candle for each one." This type of superstitious gullibility galled Calvin.

Later in life, Calvin wrote a treatise in which he satirically blasted the use of relics in the Catholic Church. "The bodies and relics of saints," he wrote, "were reduced to a kind of inventory." For a church to worry about whether it truly had in its possession the hair of John the Baptist, a tooth of the Lord, or pieces of the crown of thorns Christ wore on his way toward crucifixion, Calvin said, took away from the focus on Christ. He became highly critical of a church that used "abuses and impostures, by which the ignorant populous were cheated into the belief that the bones gathered here and there were those of saints."

To take advantage of his son's obvious intelligence, Gérard Calvin used his connections to send him to a nearby boarding school, known as the school of the Cappettes because of the *cappa* or mantle worn by the students. This small school, limited to boys, taught Calvin the humanities as well as falconry and horsemanship. In subsequent years, Calvin would use the latter skill on his many journeys across Europe.

As a youth, Calvin, like his father Gérard, forged a tight friendship with the family of Louis deHangest, lord of Montmor. One member of the deHangest family was the bishop for whom Gérard worked. Thus early on, Calvin learned to rub elbows with the upper strata of society. By careful observation, he acquired the ability to mix easily with people of a high station. With a father who was rising in the ranks of the well-to-do and a mother who came from had a noble background, it makes sense that the boy would also become, as one biographer wrote, "polished, self-assured, independent, one not out of place at the tables of the great."

Hobnobbing with the nobility might well make a young man a bit of a snob. But Calvin never showed much inclination toward putting on airs. His connection with the nobility simply allowed him to move more freely about the people in society who could help him and serve as patrons for his aims.

## LEAVING NOYON

In 1523, as Calvin finished his boarding school studies, the Bubonic plague struck, killing hundreds in Noyon. Meanwhile, war was raging to the north where the Flemish were fighting for their independence from Spain. Caught up in this war, Spanish soldiers plundered Noyon on their way to battle in the north, forcing out many people, among them, John Calvin. His father couldn't leave his work, but he insisted that his fourteen-year-old son leave to study at the University of Paris. So Calvin, accompanied by three of the deHangest boys, packed their belongings on mules and left Noyon.

The young men made this exciting trip during a crisp, sun-splashed autumn. They rode their mules past golden fields, colorful trees, tidy homes, and a patchwork of farms on the way south to Paris. After several days they spotted the windmills surrounding Paris and rode in by the north gate. Slowly they moved along the cobbled streets through the busy crowds and crossed the bridge over the Seine, and then up the hill to the university.

Later Calvin would write that it was as if a course were laid out for him, compelling him on. Although he didn't understand it then, as he rode into Paris on the cobblestone streets, he was a young man in the grip of God's guiding hand. In the words of twentieth-century German theologian Karl Barth, "God overtook Calvin like a robber . . . Calvin's God is the Lord, and to go with God he had to be God's servant." Perhaps Calvin sensed that something supernatural, just barely beyond his awareness, was stalking him, even as he rode into Paris to start school.

Having escaped both plague and plundering soldiers, after that autumn adventure traveling through the French countryside, Calvin arrived in Paris in 1523 to study at the Collège de Marchein in preparation for the university. His studies consisted of seven subjects: grammar, rhetoric, logic, arithmetic, geometry, astronomy, and music. He lodged with his father's brother Richard, a locksmith who lived near the Louvre, then a royal palace. From the start, Calvin embraced the busy, stimulating atmosphere of the school in Paris. He was in his element. It didn't seem to bother him that he never arrived home until after his daily studies ended at 8 p.m. and he had to jostle his way through the busy streets to where he was staying. Even the prostitutes hanging in doorways and the darting pickpockets didn't distract him. What did bother him, he occasionally told his uncle, was how his fellow students shirked their studies. He had seen them run wild, actually throwing stones at their teachers to taunt them.

At this time, Calvin was introduced to the Reformation as he began to read such writers as Martin Luther, whose radical ideas he was drawn to. These ideas provoked heated discussion all around the colleges and universities of Paris. At the same time, Calvin clearly recognized that there was a price to pay for embracing such radical ideas. A monk was burned alive outside the Cathedral of Notre-Dame for advancing the teachings of Martin Luther, himself a Catholic monk before he turned into a renegade reformer. We don't know if John Calvin witnessed this, or how he was specifically affected by the death. But we do know that Luther's ideas had reached Paris and were having a profound impact. Calvin may not have known quite what to make of the uproar—but he was certainly curious.

More and more, we can recognize the hand of God on Calvin's life. Once Calvin had arrived in Paris, it wasn't long before he had the good fortune to study for a short but significant time with Mathurin Codier, one of the great Latin teachers of the era, whose Latin grammar was still being used by students as late as the beginning of nineteenth century. Codier brought the ancient tongue alive for Calvin, opening entirely new vistas of reading and study for him.

Theodore Beza, one of Calvin's first biographers and a contemporary, said that Calvin could easily make friends with teachers such as Codier, "a man of great worth and erudition, and in the highest repute in almost all of the schools of France as a teacher of youth." Codier was not the kind of teacher who whipped his students. About forty-four years old at the time he taught Calvin, Codier prided himself on his ability to inspire his students to care about and to master the language that had come from the Romans. He also spoke freely of his love for Jesus Christ, a living faith that likely planted some seeds in Calvin's young mind. Having taken to this bright student, Codier closely followed Calvin's career. Eventually he became a Protestant, following his former pupil to Geneva. Because of Codier's influence, Calvin dedicated one of his commentaries to his Latin teacher. In it he spoke of what Codier had meant to him:

> When I was a child and had merely tasted the rudiments of Latin, my father sent me to Paris. There God's goodness gave you to me for a little while as preceptor, to teach me the true way to learn so that I might continue with greater profit. . . . I enjoyed your teaching for only a little space. . . . Yet I was so helped by you that whatever progress I have made since I gladly ascribe to you.

Beza, who knew Calvin for many years and would take over the work in Geneva when Calvin died, says that Calvin was successful in all of his studies from the start and that he "so profited that he left his fellow students in the grammar course behind and was promoted to dialectics and the study of other so-called arts." Even at an early age, he "was remarkably religious, and was also a strict censor of every thing vicious in his companions. This I remember to have heard from some Catholics, unexceptional witnesses, many years after he had risen to celebrity." Calvin's stodgy attitude earned him the grammatical title the "Accusative Case" from his peers.

We can picture Calvin during these years as a slender, stoop-shouldered, intense, and solitary youth who was fascinated by the world of ideas. At the same time, he could show an outgoing personality, especially with his teachers and mentors. Perhaps because he excelled in his studies, Calvin soon transferred to another college at the University of Paris.

The Collège de Montaigu was dark and dreary, and the food was horrible. It was situated in the midst of a maze of dirty, narrow streets, surrounded by monasteries, churches, chapels, bookstores, and brothels. Sewage seeped in the streets, rolling downhill onto the college grounds, making the trips back and forth to school less than pleasant. But Calvin soldiered on. Though the demands on him were many, he remained in generally good spirits, able to make friends and keep friends whose interest in him must have come from his personality and approach to life. While not especially humorous, Calvin was an eager conversationalist and was dependable and supportive to his friends.

The schedule at college was backbreaking. Biographers tell us that Calvin normally rose about 4 a.m. to pray, followed by a lecture, and then required daily attendance at Mass. After Mass came breakfast, and then from eight until ten a class and discussion, followed at eleven by lunch, accompanied by readings from the Bible or the recitation of the life of a saint, followed by prayers and college announcements. After the meal students discussed the morning class. Then there was a rest period and another class. Vespers came after that, followed by discussion of the afternoon class. Supper and its attendant readings merged into more discussion, attendance at chapel and bedtime at eight in winter or nine in the summer.

Teachers at the college tended to be dull and dour, and many held firmly to the orthodox teachings of Catholicism. But this was the school that Erasmus, one of Calvin's heroes, had attended a few years earlier, and soon after Calvin left, Ignatius Loyola, founder of the Jesuit order, studied there as well. And it was here that Calvin began in earnest his studies in the arts, with the idea of one day becoming a priest.

The school year began on October 1 and ended in July when Calvin would return to Noyon for vacation. Calvin prospered in his studies at the college and moved forward quickly to study philosophy and dialectics, the study of putting words to one's ideas and to be able to express them, often in public debate. This discipline certainly helped to hone the logical mind that enabled Calvin to write and preach in ways that connected with many who read or listened to him.

Calvin eagerly began to read the writings of Augustine of Hippo, the fifth-century Catholic theologian who came to God after a great struggle.

With his background in Latin, Calvin was able to read Augustine in the original. From these writings he gained a powerful sense of the role Jesus Christ—and the love of God—should play in one's faith. Erasmus's ideas, calling for radical change in the church, also had a strong influence on Calvin. But the college itself wasn't open to the new ideas of men like Martin Luther that by then were sweeping Germany. Instead the focus was on the teachings of the schoolmen of the later Middle Ages. "[Calvin] was taught to think in a room with the windows shut; no breath of air came in from the outside to disturb the atmosphere," said one biographer.

Although Calvin never really wrote about this time in college, the strict life of prayer and study surely must have had an impact his relationship with God. It's worth remembering once again that Calvin was not a born critic of the Roman Catholic Church—rather, he was drawn to it and remained a dedicated Catholic during these years of study.

# Chapter 3

# CLAIMED BY GOD

A fter four long years at Collège de Montaigu, just as he was graduating with a degree in arts, Calvin received an unexpected letter from his father telling him to forget being a priest. He was to go to Orléans to study law and engage in a career that would have more prestige and make him a better living. Priests, especially those who ran parishes, were barely more than paupers. The letter came at a time when Gérard Calvin was feuding over money matters with Catholic authorities in Noyon and very possibly losing his grasp on his faith.

Ever the dutiful son, Calvin did as he was told and went to Orléans to study law. There he flourished in what turned out to be much a freer atmosphere. He took law classes, memorizing canon law and common law with characteristic enthusiasm, continuing the rigorous study habits he'd developed in college. Soon he was speaking out in class, defending some laws and criticizing others. He thought quickly on his feet and wasn't afraid to debate others, often convincing opponents of his point of view. Eventually he did so well that he was asked to take the place of an instructor or two when they couldn't make it to class.

While at Orléans, Calvin spent time with Pierre Olivétan, his cousin and an eventual convert to Protestantism. This gave him the opportunity to talk at length to his relative about a range of ideas, including this growing Reformation movement that Calvin found increasingly attractive. When Olivétan published a Bible in French in 1535, Calvin contributed a preface in Latin describing Olivétan as a relative and an intimate friend.

During this period, particularly during his final years of college, Calvin heard news of the bloody purges being launched against Lutherans in France and elsewhere. Believers were often branded as heretics and burned, decapitated, or sometimes torn apart by angry mobs. A young man with a shy and sensitive disposition, Calvin would have been deeply disturbed to think of this carnage occurring over religious belief. Nevertheless, he didn't stop reading and talking to others about this new approach to faith. Slowly but surely, the belief system of the Roman Catholic Church of his day was losing its grip on him. Increasingly, he saw Catholicism in the same way as Luther and others: its practices had become antiquated, and church officials wielded far too much political and religious power. Calvin and his friends began to see Catholicism as a repressive religion rather than one that freed a person to come closer to God.

Calvin enjoyed the friendship of a select circle of people with whom he could talk openly and who understood the ideas he was wrestling with. These friends were struggling as well, and they appreciated the perceptive ways in which Calvin spoke about matters of faith. But when they attended parties or got involved in revelry, Calvin held back. Instead of rollicking with the other students, he studied hard, read deeply, and stayed up much of the night mulling over and making sure he grasped what he had read. For this reason he seemed distant and judgmental to some, and yet warmly open, although easily offended, with others. Some biographers say this was when Calvin began the hard-driving intellectual and physical habits that led to a series of serious medical problems. He didn't pay much attention to the food he ate when he got around to eating, and his favorite forms of "exercise" were writing and an occasional walk.

Calvin seemed destined for the sedate life of the scholar and writer, and he certainly saw himself as a man of letters. And yet, Calvin wrote, he wasn't necessarily the one making the decisions in his life. By now, the inklings he had felt for a long while were becoming an overwhelming urge to do the will of God. Constantly at odds with himself, Calvin wanted seclusion and peace, but he also felt God's insistent claim on his life. "While my one great object was to live in seclusion without being known, God so led me through different turnings and changes that he never permitted me to rest in any place, until, in spite of my natural disposition, he brought me forth to public notice."

Calvin was a man always in tension, driven forward by his mind and perhaps held back by his shy personality. But Calvin liked to preach even when he was in law school. Inspired and passionate about his newfound faith, he gave sermons to small groups of friends, letting them know what he was learning outside of his normal studies. Whether he had fully converted to Protestantism at this time is unclear. Yet his time as a law student, away from the colleges in Paris, was clearly a time of spiritual awakening. Once he had settled into this new line of study, he felt set free. Without having known it, his early life had been something of a prison. He'd performed well in school and college, but as he looked back, what he had been taught felt empty and academic—at odds with sacred stirrings in his heart.

Calvin loved law school. And so while these spiritual stirrings increased in Orléans, he continued to become schooled in the basics of the law. He was taught the laws governing the disposal of rain water, rights of way, leases, purchase and possession, marriage and divorce, and inheritance. Much of this came from the accumulated canon law of the Catholic Church, as well as laws as they applied to certain communities. His legal studies also helped teach him to prepare and argue cases. This sharpened his abilities as a would-be lawyer and gave him a view of the messy secular world beyond the walls of the academy. All this would flower in later life when he helped fashion both the religious and civil life of Geneva.

## LOOKING FOR DIRECTION

Next Calvin did what many law students of his era did: he enrolled in another school, hoping for a wider range of learning. Students often moved from college to college, seeking to study under the best teachers. Calvin left Orléans in the autumn of 1529 to study under a famous Italian legal scholar, Andrea Alciati, at Bourges. He also studied Greek under Melchior Wolmar, a respected churchman and teacher who played a key role in bolstering Calvin's attention to new ideas of such reformers as Martin Luther. In part through Wolmar, Calvin began to hear about new translations from the ancient Greek and jumped at the chance to read large portions of the Bible. Learning Greek, he became familiar with the ancient philosophers, along with the early church fathers. These writings transformed his worldview and helped to revolutionize his way of thinking. Calvin would later dedicate a book to Wolmar with the words: "Nothing has greater weight with me than the memory of when I was sent by my father to study civil law. Under your direction and tuition I added to the study of law Greek literature, of which you were then a celebrated professor." Greek opened his eyes even more widely to the world of the ancients, to a world much closer to the truths that Calvin sought.

He graduated easily from law school, even as he continued to read the works of Augustine and the Roman philosopher and ethicist Seneca, about whom he was writing a book. Convinced that he didn't want to work as a lawyer, he thought for a time of entering a monastery. There he could spend his days in prayer and worship and study without being interrupted by the ongoing clamor of the world. But Calvin had his doubts: "I had read enough of a book by an ex-friar named Francois Rabelais . . . to be discouraged at the absence of any intellectuality in monasteries, and the lechery and so on that were habitual with a large number of monks." Ruling out the monastery, he couldn't quite decide what else to do. Most likely, Calvin still held hopes that the church of his youth could change, and he with it. Yet he could see that with the foment of change all around, it was quickly becoming too late to reform the church from within. The church hierarchy was too lost in its own self-preservation.

Calvin also became friends with Marguerite d'Angoulême, sister of the French king and a great sympathizer with those trying to reform the Catholic Church. She was a protector and defender of more open-minded scholars, offering many of them asylum or encouragement, and even helping to fund them. Calvin appreciated that someone of her station would offer support. In gratitude he wrote an article praising a play she had written or promoted that had been criticized.

Entering his early twenties, the young Calvin felt the itch of ambition, along with a sense that his intellect could take him places. Still, he had no clear sense of direction. "O Christ," he prayed, "have you forgotten me?" Head down, Calvin walked the streets, murmuring to himself, at loose ends. If he had any aspirations of substance, they revolved around writing—especially the book he was writing about Seneca. Maybe this could propel him into the scholarly circles in which he could envision himself participating. At the same time, racked by doubt and fear, Calvin wondered if he had any real talent for a literary life. The young man felt a strange disconnection between himself and much that he had experienced up until that time. His mind wound itself in circles, but he kept coming back to the notion that he was destined to be a writer. Even as he struggled with these questions, he continued to make progress on his book.

In the spring of 1531, Calvin traveled to Paris, checking out publishers for his book on Seneca. To his dismay, no one seemed interested. He may also have been investigating further studies at one of the universities. While there, he had the chance to write his first published piece—the preface to a book written by his friend Nicholas du Chemin. Calvin's friend had penned a treatise called *Antapologia*, a rebuttal to a book written by Andrea Alciati, the law professor under whom both had studied in Bourges. Although the Italian was a good lawyer and worth listening to, he was also pompous, vain, and even coarse; someone who talked too much of himself and his own ideas and showed his contempt for the French judiciary. Calvin had no problem praising his friend's treatise, thus making it clear that he too had problems with Alciati and his often too urbane ideas.

## A FATHER'S DEATH

After writing the preface for his friend's treatise, Calvin learned that his father had fallen ill and returned to Noyon. It was clear that his father was near the end, even as he battled the illness for several days. As his father rallied and then waned, Calvin walked the rooms of the house. There was little he could do but watch and wait. He knew his father would soon be gone, and that he should try to be tender. In a letter to a friend at this time, he expressed annoyance at having to be in Noyon at this time. Although some scholars see this as proof that he was insensitive and hated his fater, it is hard to believe that Calvin was simply callous and uncaring. We can imagine the mixture of emotions Calvin must have felt: frustrated at being trapped at his father's bedside when he had so much to do, but also feeling helpless that he couldn't do more to help the old man. Calvin probably had much to say to his father that he could never put into words. Finally, the end came. The reality of Gérard's death seemed hard for Calvin to grasp. But as if to prove his loyalty to his father, Calvin remained in Noyon for a few weeks to take care of family business.

Because of a dispute between Calvin's father and church authorities that involved mismanagement of money, the church refused Gérard a holy burial. John's brother Charles intervened, however, telling church leaders that his father deserved better. John, the newly minted lawyer, also made the case for his father, arguing that Gérard had given the best years of his life to the church. Finally, church authorities were persuaded—or simply worn down by the brothers—to have Gérard buried near the cathedral in town. Maybe they hashed out an agreement—a decent burial in exchange for money, because Charles and John also spent time trying to figure out the financial mess their father had gotten into and then returned the funds to the church. Calvin spent about a month in his hometown, leaving once to conduct a service in the little chapel of Pont-l'Evêque, where his father was born and where John was still the chaplain, in name and salary. Finally he set off again for Paris, leaving the old life of Noyon behind and trudging toward what he desperately hoped would be a new and fuller life for himself.

As he got further from Noyon and closer to Paris, Calvin began to feel a powerful sense of liberation. No longer would his father pressure him to practice law. Instead, he was free to pursue his heart's desire—further study of the classics, the life of a humanist writer and scholar. Once he reached Paris, Calvin enrolled in the Collège de Fortet. He began studying Greek and Hebrew under very competent teachers. Finally Calvin seems to have truly engaged the questions that had been haunting him for so long. He thought about all that he had been reading about Luther and the other reformers. He felt God calling him to face the truth—Catholicism had become to him more a superstition than a faith he could embrace. He had felt that acutely in Noyon, especially when he and Charles were arguing with Catholic authorities over what were, in the end, relatively petty temporal matters. Church officials seemed to care much more for what was contained in his father's bank account than in his soul as he died.

## THE CASE FOR PROTESTANTISM

It's impossible to give a date for Calvin's conversion. We know, for instance, that even in 1531 he was still on the fence. One of Calvin's friends asked him at that time to talk his sister out of entering a Catholic convent. Calvin did visit his sister, but he did not demand that she renounce the

Roman Catholic Church. As if also giving advice to himself, he simply told her to think carefully about what she wanted to do for her future. This might imply that Calvin hadn't yet turned his back on the church. But it could also mean that he was the type of young man who believed others should make their own decisions. God's work was mysterious, and Calvin believed it wasn't really his job to try to convert someone else.

During this time, Calvin started reading more deeply in the Bible, searching for answers, especially about the life of Christ. The story of Jesus affected him in a profound way. In Christ, he found a person who was holy and who also engaged people. Calvin saw in Jesus a man who was also God. Here was a model for his life and the life of others. Gradually his heart became overwhelmed with love for the one who accepted death on a cross to pay the price for all the sins of the world. Calvin left no record of whether he had a moment of blinding insight and acceptance of his salvation through Christ. Indeed, if there was such a moment, Calvin likely would have been uncomfortable talking about it anyway. To him it seemed to be a profoundly private matter—the culmination of a long process of being won over and then of giving himself over. Characteristically, Calvin wrote of the profound change without giving the details. "I indeed had learned to worship thee as my God," he wrote later on in life. "But since the true way to worship thee utterly eluded me, I stumbled at the very threshold."

When Calvin specifically walked through that threshold of faith, he doesn't say. We don't know whether his conversion was sudden or a more gradual process in which he began to see more clearly the truths in the Bible and accepted them without fanfare. It is clear, however, that at this point in his life Calvin did change. He realized that he would need to get more thoroughly involved in reforming the Catholic Church, and especially try to bring this new faith to his beloved France. Later, in the introduction to his *Commentary on the Psalms*, he wrote: "God drew me from obscure and lowly beginnings and conferred on me that most notable office of herald and minister of the Gospel. . . . What happened first was that by an unexpected conversion he tamed to teachableness a mind . . . strongly devoted to the superstitions of the Papacy."

In a letter in which he made the case for Protestantism to the noted Catholic scholar Jacopo Sadoleto several years later, Calvin imagines what this new faith might mean to the average pastor. Speaking in the voice of his fictional pastor, but likely also describing himself, Calvin wrote, "God showed me that there is no source of truth that can be compared to the Bible. I could not find peace of conscience. . . . Then all of a sudden a new faith made its appearance which did not lead us away from 'the Christian profession,' but one 'which brought it back to its fountainhead.'" Clearly Calvin considered his conversion as a sovereign work of God.

## THE FIRST PUBLICATION

It was also during this period of struggle and eventual enlightenment that Calvin made the decision to self-publish his first book, the commentary on Seneca's *De Clementia*—"On Clemency." Since no publisher seemed to want it, he took the leap and published it himself. And as he was still receiving money for his studies from the church in Noyon, Calvin had some funds to spare. Although having to revert to a "vanity press" hurt him, he tried to drum up recognition for his first publication, writing his friends to ask them to buy his book, and anxiously checking in bookstores to see if they were carrying it. Disappointingly, most were not. Readers were impressed by the clarity of his writing and the depth of his scholarship, but sales were dismal.

Seneca, the subject of Calvin's book, was a Stoic philosopher in the time of Emperor Nero. He wrote his book trying to convince Nero, who was not known for his clemency, to go easier on his subjects. Calvin was attracted to Seneca's deep sense of ethical principle. So Calvin's book wasn't a religious book but a book about morals and ethics. He wrote as a humanist about the harmonious life of a Stoic philosopher who trained himself to react to the world with a sense of balance formed by careful thought and reading. Stoicism downplayed the role of emotion and encouraged the philosopher to make his decisions as unemotionally as possible. It had to do, Calvin wrote, with listening and adhering to one's conscience. It is hard to say whether Calvin believed in this sense of hardy individualism at that point in his life. Certainly later on, he did not. Adhering to the will of God, being in service to God, were the hallmarks of what he would teach and write about in a relatively short time. One could argue, though, that Calvin was a Stoic for God. His sensitive conscience was a conduit through which the Lord spoke and guided him. Later Calvin would often say that even his conscience was not his own. He had allowed God to take it—it was a conscience formed by the Holy Spirit.

In this work on Seneca, Calvin tried to do a little fencing with his hero, Erasmus, taking the famous and admired Catholic radical to task for not really understanding the ideas and purposes of Seneca in the book Erasmus had written about him. While Calvin admired Erasmus's call for a return to exploring the early texts of the church, he thought Erasmus had been too hard on the Roman Stoic philosopher. It's worth noting, however, that Erasmus himself said he didn't have it all right, and that another book expounding on his translation of Seneca might be a good idea. Calvin may have thought that he could spark a career by taking Erasmus up on his challenge with a more in-depth and scholarly look at Seneca's work. If that was his hope, it was not to be. In fact, there may have even been a bit of a backlash because this young upstart had had the temerity to face off with the great Erasmus. The book's lucid writing and scholarly research did win him a minor reputation, but rather than making a big splash, Calvin's book only turned out to be a small ripple.

# Chapter 4

# A MAN ON THE RUN

Perhaps hoping for a respite from his attempt to make it as a man of letters, Calvin took a short trip to Orléans and then went back home to Noyon to attend a meeting of the chapter of clergy, a way for him to maintain his stipend before returning to Paris. During this period, the city was experiencing increasingly tense conflicts between Catholics and Protestants. Calvin met and talked with many people about the basics of faith, and of the things he was starting to see by reading the Bible. Among those he befriended, found lodging with, and learned from was a well-to-do cloth merchant named Estienne de la Forge. The merchant had already made a break in his heart from the Catholic Church. Although wary of causing too much controversy by being too public, he spoke to Calvin and others about his new religious convictions. These people often gathered in cellars, back alleys, and homes to talk about their new, emerging faith. They even held services at which Calvin sometimes officiated and preached, apparently with great energy.

Clearly Calvin was becoming less furtive about his faith and was emerging as a leader. Yet he did it slowly and carefully. A child of the Catholic Church, he fervently wished at times that it would awaken and reform itself. At the same time, he was growing to dislike, even hate, the pope and all that he represented to a somnolent church.

Although he often spoke of taking on such tasks as preaching with the greatest reluctance, his actions speak for themselves as he began to preach with conviction, vigor, and growing boldness. Those who attended these hidden services say Calvin always concluded his preaching with the words of St. Paul, "If God be for us, who can be against us?" Such certainty solidified in Calvin, and he found himself increasingly invested in a movement that spoke to the issues that people faced in his day.

Among Calvin's many friends at this time was Nicholas Cop, son of the physician to the king. Cop was something of a rabble-rouser, in a clever and highly intellectual way. Calvin and Cop didn't get along at first. They circled one another, checking out the other's ideas and beliefs. When convinced that they were spiritual kin, they became friends who spent a great deal of time talking and perhaps even plotting, some scholars say.

Cop, a learned scholar, was elected rector at the University of Paris and was asked to give the address on All Saints Day of 1533 that marked the beginning of the academic year. Many people from the university gathered in the Church of Mathurins to hear what Cop had to say. Doubtless Calvin was sitting among those gathered in the church as Cop spoke, mincing few words about the cobwebs in which Catholicism was entangled. From the very start of his address, he criticized his conservative theological colleagues, claiming that these faculty members wasted their time on small, inconsequential matters: they "contend perpetually about trifles" and neglect true Christian philosophy. He went on to talk about Christ's Sermon on the Mount and Christ's blessing on the peacemakers. This crucial passage in the Bible set out the practical, world-changing theology that Christ espoused. "Would that in this our unhappy age we restore peace in the Church by the Word rather than the sword," Cop said. Essentially, he preached about the Beatitudes. He spoke of salvation in Jesus who said, "Blessed are they who are persecuted." Cop didn't have to spell out who was being persecuted or who was doing the persecuting. Boldly Cop took his fellow professors—and the institution for which they taught—to task. He closed his presentation by fervently asking God to open "our minds that we may believe in the Gospel."

We don't know how Calvin reacted as Cop spoke. Some scholars claim that Calvin had written a large part of the speech or at the very least was in on the early drafts. In any case, Calvin believed every word that Cop spoke. At the same time, he must have listened to the speech with some anxiety, wondering how it would go over. He didn't have to wait long to find out. There was a great buzzing among the monks, priests, and professors as they discussed and debated this sermon, which they realized was aimed at them and at the Catholic Church. Cop had in essence given a manifesto on behalf of Protestantism, and they were in part his foil. They couldn't ignore this bold and forthright challenge to the Catholic Church—especially as it came from their new rector. An uproar of criticism mounted in the days after Cop spoke, and he was called to defend his speech before city officials. Cop learned that there was a good chance that, regardless of what he said, he would be put in jail, and from there even sentenced to death. So he quickly left town.

Cop did not tell Calvin that he was leaving, which angered and worried Calvin. If Cop was in danger, would he also be singled out as a troublemaker? Torn, Calvin wondered if he should follow. He wanted to stay and keep out of harm's way in this city where he had made many friends, especially among the underground church. Then Calvin was alerted that the Paris authorities believed he was involved in drafting Cop's address, and that they wanted to arrest him. This warning, however, came pretty late in the day—just before the authorities came stomping up to his upstairs apartment. Listening to them come closer, Calvin quickly changed his clothes, tied together some bed sheets to make a ladder, and slipped out of his apartment. Dressed in the nondescript garb of a farm boy, he hustled out of town.

Arriving too late, the authorities ransacked his apartment. Among other things, they confiscated many of his youthful letters, perhaps to use as evidence once they caught up with him. We don't know what these letters contained, and they never surfaced again.

It's not clear where Calvin went for next two or three weeks, but the hurried flight set the tone for the next stage of his life. Constant movement and flight would be a big part of his life for the next several years. We do know that Calvin, once assured that the danger for him had passed, wasn't gone long. He was back in Paris for a short time in December. He decided to lie low, aware that the anti-Protestant atmosphere was heating up—literally. So-called heretics were being burned at the stake. Calvin nonetheless met with friends, wondering what he should do next. His new-found faith was growing and he felt compelled to stand by it. His friend, the merchant de la Forge, apparently told Calvin to leave: the situation was getting out of control.

In these dangerous circumstances, it was hard to tell who was a friend and who was a foe. Some "supporters" were talking to the authorities, revealing where the Protestants were meeting. Things took on an added intensity when opposing groups—Catholics on one side and Protestants on the other—began fighting in the streets. Blood flowed. Bones were broken. The fight over which would be the true church in Paris, and in France, had begun in earnest.

Calvin knew he had to get out. It is said that before leaving Paris, at the urging of his friend de la Forge, Calvin went to meet and talk to a young man of Anabaptist leanings. This man was Servetus, a Spanish physician who would play a tragic role much later in Calvin's life. Calvin, feeling ever more pulled toward the pastorate, probably wanted to steer Servetus away from his wrongheaded thinking on such matters as the Trinity. Servetus, however, didn't veer from his path. The two would correspond in later years as Calvin kept trying to amend his thinking.

## THE WANDERING FUGITIVE

In January of 1534, Calvin left Paris, assuming the life of a wandering fugitive. He spent the better part of the next three years trying to stay concealed. Convinced that things were only going to get worse for the reformers, he began living under assumed names. One of his first stops revealed God's protecting hand. He was given refuge in the town of Angoulême in the home of a friend, Louis du Tillet, the well-heeled son of the nobleman who also happened to be the canon of the Cathedral of Angoulême. Along with a safe place to stay, Calvin was given access to the extensive library in du Tillet's home, which may have contained three or four thousand books and manuscripts. Calvin delved deeply into this treasure trove of learning. He must have felt that he was where he needed to be, in a library, able to read and research and write to his heart's content. To help pay for his lodging, he is said to have taught du Tillet Greek.

Most scholars think that it was here that Calvin started to sketch the outline for his most famous work, *The Institutes of the Christian Faith*. He wanted to put together a book that clearly explained the beliefs of the reformers. But the young man grew restless. Even though he had access to books and manuscripts, he had questions that weren't being answered in the comfort of his friend's library. Perhaps the things he read, in a place of literary quiet and reflection, pushed him forward. He felt compelled to keep seeking. He needed more than what he could find on printed paper.

Wanting to talk to someone about the need for reforming the Catholic Church, Calvin chose to visit Jacques Lefèvre, one of the leaders of the humanistic reformers of France. Then living under the protection of King Francis I in Nerac, in southwestern France, Lefèvre was a well-known, aging Catholic theologian who had been calling for reform in his many writings, some of which the Catholic Church had called heretical. It is probable that Calvin met with Lefèvre in early April of 1534, about the same time the revised edition of Lefèvre's translation of the Bible into French was published in Antwerp.

Born in 1455, Lefèvre was seventy-nine years old, an amazing age at that time. Bent and wrinkled, he invited the young man inside and they talked. Both hailed from the region of Picardy, which helped bond them together. Not much is known about the meeting, but Lefèvre seems to have pushed Calvin over the edge into the life of a committed reformer and fierce prophet for the Bible. As he reminisced about his own varied and well-traveled life, the old reformer may have told the young one that trying to reform the Roman church from within was not going to work; a bold new approach was needed. Lefèvre had loved the church and had tried to work within the system to bring the saving message of Jesus. But Catholic authorities blocked him at every turn, calling into question his emphasis on faith in Christ alone, and banning and burning his books. Over time, it had become clear to him that the church was more interested in its own survival and growth than in feeding the Word of God to God's people.

We can imagine the frail old man leaning close and offering some disturbing and yet also uplifting words before Calvin got up to go. Feed the people, he may have said. Forget the trappings of power; give people the straight truth for which they hunger. He is said to have told Calvin that he had a big task in front of him, and that he was an instrument of God, chosen to bring Protestantism to France. It was as if the old theologian were passing on the mantle of change and charging the younger man with accomplishing what Lefèvre had been unable to do. Calvin must have felt as if the hand of God had reached down and snatched him up for his own purposes. The old man was telling Calvin that the time had come to make the break. These were things Calvin had already concluded. But coming from the mouth of the aging priest, these words inspired him to act.

## A FINAL BREAK WITH THE CATHOLIC CHURCH

A month or so after meeting with Lefèvre, Calvin made the final break with the Catholic Church. Determined as never before, he returned to Noyon to formally renounce his stipend that had for many years supported him as a would-be priest for study and research. We don't know if he did this in a public manner, drawing attention to the act, or if he quietly stopped in an office and signed a form. Either way, he formally rid himself of the final vestiges of the Catholic Church that clung to him. Once again Calvin was following his conscience, as he did throughout his life. For it was through conscience that God spoke most forcefully. By now, Calvin was beginning to fully understand that his life and aspirations were not really his own. God was making it clear to him—at times through such men as Lefèvre—that it was time to leave the Catholic Church and its superstitions behind.

Calvin remained in Noyon for a while, possibly to talk with his older brother, Charles, against whom charges of heresy had been lodged. Charles too had been a recipient of the church's funding and actually became a priest at one time. Ultimately, though, he left the priesthood, got married, and quarreled so much with Catholic officials that they excommunicated him. Perhaps John wanted to help him and talk about his new faith. It is doubtful that Charles listened, though, because his life continued to spiral downward. There is some evidence that John was thrown into jail at this time by the officials of Noyon, perhaps because he had broken with the church that had supported him so generously. We will never know for certain what happened during this final visit to Noyon.

After he left Noyon, Calvin ended up in Poitiers, France, with du Tillet. Calvin stayed at the home of a friend of du Tillet, the prior of a nearby monastery called Trois-Moutiers, who engaged Calvin in conversation about the new ideas of the Protestant faith. The two had lengthy, even heated exchanges. At some point, the prior mentioned to Calvin that formal discussions were occurring at the University of Poitiers about the bevy of new ideas. The university prided itself on its willingness to explore any idea that seemed to have substance. So Calvin went one day to listen in on the talk. What he heard troubled him. The conversation was not opened-ended at all: instead the focus was on why the Catholic Church should remain supreme. Listening, Calvin grew troubled, realizing that these highly educated people at the University of Poitiers, the second oldest university in France, really didn't understand the changes that Luther and others, like himself, were advocating. Unable to contain himself, he stood and gave the professors and others an impromptu speech about the new ideas and how they differed from the teachings of the Catholic Church. Calvin's speech won admirers and critics.

The admirers started stopping by to talk to Calvin. Often they often strolled through a nearby garden and spoke about the momentous changes in their thinking. One of the topics of discussion was the Lord's Supper—a core sacrament that stood at the heart of the gospel, as well as the teaching of the Catholic Church. Calvin talked of the Lord's Supper being more than a symbol, but less than consuming the actual body and blood of Christ. Those who heard Calvin criticizing the traditional understanding of the sacrament and advocating another approach gathered to discuss Calvin's views. Soon rumors began to fly that Calvin and the others were in danger of being attacked as they walked through the garden and held their discussion on the new faith. Calvin even heard that the police might arrest him. To avoid the possibility of trouble, Calvin and his friends decided to take a lower profile approach. They needed to be less public. After some discussion, they decided on a suitable place to meet: a set of caves on the outskirts of a nearby town known as Benedict's Caves. It was a lovely place, with the waters of the Clain River flowing by.

At the appointed time, Calvin joined others who took a footpath through the nearby town and gathered in the area that housed the caves. For secrecy's sake, they slipped into one of the largest caves to hear Calvin expound on the primacy of the Bible and the value of having Christ in one's heart. "Better to be deprived of everything and possess Christ," Calvin said to the crowd. "If the ship is in danger, the sailors throw everything overboard, that they may reach the port in safety. Do likewise. Riches, honors, rank, outward respect—all should be sacrificed to possess Christ. He is our blessedness." Along with this message, Calvin denounced the Catholic Mass as an abomination. The group met elsewhere in Poitiers, often in quiet, out-of-the-way homes or in a country house outside of town.

After a time, though, it became clear to Calvin that the Catholic forces in the community were coalescing against him; he and du Tillet would need to move on. But before leaving Poitiers, Calvin held a communion service with friends in the cave that was becoming known as Calvin's Grotto. Calvin developed a liturgy for this service that was similar to the liturgy he would write for the churches of Geneva and Strasbourg, and he performed it with dignity and sincerity. In the dim, wet cave, surrounded by friends, Calvin stood behind a large rock that served as the table. He read a passage from the Gospels about the Lord's Supper, describing the institution of the sacrament, and again denouncing the Roman Mass. According to one of Calvin's biographers, this may have been one of the first Reformed services in France. Calvin read from Mark's gospel narrative of the Last Supper. With the eyes of his friends on him, Calvin read, "While they were eating, Jesus took bread, gave thanks and broke it, and gave it to his disciples, saying, 'Take it; this is my body.'" After reading from Scripture, Calvin invited his friends to the table. "Brethren," he said, "let us eat the Lord's bread in the memory of his death and passion."

Taking the bread in hand, Calvin broke it into smaller pieces and gave them to his friends, who ate in silence and then drank the wine. When the Lord's Supper was finished, Calvin offered words of thanksgiving, and everyone said the Lord's Prayer and the Apostle's Creed in Latin. It was a moving, low-key service, says one of Calvin's biographers. "In this fashion, it may be believed, Calvin ministered to the little community, and he justified his rejection to the Roman worship by an appeal the Scriptures."

## THE POWER OF THE WORD

Leaving Poitiers, Calvin traveled with du Tillet to Orléans. By now, thoroughly committed to reforming the church, he wanted to use his writing talent to advance the cause. The freelance writer of the book about Seneca now turned his full attention and talents to theology. Over a period of time, sketching words as he went, Calvin finished his first theological work: *Psychopanychia*. In it, he refuted a doctrine promulgated by the Anabaptists, a controversial group that taught the necessity of re-baptism for those who wanted to truly be Christians. Calvin had a special dislike of the Anabaptist approach. In his opinion, they were bending Scripture to their own purposes. In addition, their failure to place enough emphasis on the need for church discipline, led, Calvin believed, to moral laxness. They seemed to lack a sense of the significance of one, universal church under God. He also took on the doctrine of "soul sleep," a belief that the soul sleeps unconsciously between the death of the body and its resurrection on Judgment Day. Calvin argued that the soul survives the body and is then reunited with it at the time of the resurrection. This wasn't an earth-shattering issue, but Calvin felt compelled to set the Anabaptists straight. Although he finished the book in 1534, not too long after leaving Poitiers, it was not published until 1542.

From Orléans, once again accompanied by du Tillet, Calvin traveled by horse toward Basel in what is now Switzerland, perhaps because his friend Nicholas Cop was living there. By now, Calvin was feeling a compelling need to pass on what he knew and thought about the new faith. His uncertainty of a year or two ago was gone. Calvin must have taken some pleasure in finally knowing which way his life would lead. He and du Tillet likely talked about some of this as they rode together. It might have been an enjoyable trip—that is, until one night a servant stole their money and one of the horses. Fortunately, another servant had money to pay for food and lodging and the friends pressed on, arriving in Basel at the beginning of 1535.

As he settled into what he hoped would become a fairly sedate life in a town that had already embraced the Reformation, Calvin got word of violence and anti-Protestant riots in Paris. The turmoil came in the aftermath of the infamous Night of Placards. On this night, Protestants plastered the city with placards denouncing the Catholic Mass. One of the Protestants tacking up placards made it to the palace of King Francis I and brazenly placed one on his door. When the king awoke and discovered this loathsome placard on his door, he flew into a rage. He called for heads to roll and bodies to be burned. Soon the king's men were carrying out his orders, rounding up as many of these renegade Protestants as possible and carrying out the king's orders to kill them.

Among those killed was Calvin's friend, the merchant Estienne de la Forge. Shattered, Calvin considered returning to Paris to confront those who had murdered his friend. He recalled the long hours he had spent talking about his new faith with de la Forge and his family. Eventually deciding it was best that he stay away from Paris, Calvin no doubt dropped to his knees in prayer, pouring out his sorrow at losing his friend and petitioning God for answers.

It didn't take long before the answer came. Calvin knew the direction his grief and anger were to take. He realized he could use these emotions, spurred by the outburst of violence, to return to his book, *The Institutes*. The greatest gift he could lend to the cause, he realized, was in writing. He would write in order to "vindicate from unjust affront my brethren whose death was precious in the sight of the Lord; and, next that some sorrow and anxiety should move foreign peoples, since the same sufferings threatened many." He hoped that through this book he could help explain this new religion in a way that might quell the violence being perpetrated on his friends and fellow believers in Paris.

Eager now to put into clear writing the meaning of this great movement of God, the scholar turned apologist, plunging ahead with characteristic passion and commitment. By this time in his life Calvin was starting to be battered by bad health, including headaches and chronic indigestion, probably the result of parasites. But he saw these as small challenges compared to the divine calling he had been given. Calvin would write that he could not keep his pen quiet. "I felt that my silence would be treachery and that I should oppose with all my might—not only lest the undeserved shedding of the innocent blood of holy martyrs should be concealed by a false report, but also lest they should go on in the future to whatever slaughter they pleased without arousing the pity of any."

Now living quietly in the home of a widow in Basel, he launched back into his *Institutes*. Feeling as if he had become a conduit for God's words, Calvin used his drive and burning intelligence to describe how God worked in the world, and to point out how this new breed of believers was seeking truth, not trouble. While he may have blanched to think that his effort would bring publicity and likely more scorn, Calvin shoved aside the constant anxiety that seemed to plague him. At this point in his life, Calvin clearly saw that he had a higher purpose. He believed strongly that God was using him as a prophet charged with the duty of refreshing and renewing the church.

Writing feverishly and drawing on his training as a humanist and a lawyer, Calvin finished page after page of the *Institutes*.

From the very beginning, Calvin displayed the fruits of his humanist education by painting the Christian faith on the broadest possible canvas. "Nearly all the wisdom we possess, that is to say, true and sound wisdom, consists of two parts: the knowledge of God and of ourselves." This idea is in harmony with those of even pagan Greek philosophers such as Plato. But Calvin quickly moved on to the impossibility of achieving any real knowledge of God on our own and, as a result, failing to truly know ourselves. Inside every person, he said, is the "seed of religion," an innate sense of the reality of God, planted in their hearts by the Creator. Going on to quote the ancient philosophers Diagorus, Cicero, and Plato, Calvin showed how even these pagans understood that the "worship of God alone renders men higher than the brutes, and through it alone they aspire to immortality."

Training his pen like a cannon on the Catholic Church, Calvin went on to discredit the sacraments of Confirmation, Penance, Extreme Unction, Holy Orders, and Marriage. In order to be a sacrament, Calvin argued, a rite must be commanded by Christ and revealed clearly in Scripture—a standard all of these traditional Catholic sacraments failed to meet. Only baptism and the Lord's Supper, specifically commanded by Christ in the Bible, met Calvin's criteria.

Calvin was also concerned that believers understand and practice these two sacraments in a way that pointed to their real meaning. In the *Institutes*, Calvin characteristically attacked the way in which the Catholic Church turned baptism almost into a farce: "How much better would it be to omit from baptism all theatrical pomp, which dazzles the eyes of the simple and deadens their minds." He argued for a simple practice of baptism, through sprinkling or immersion, performed before the entire church, and then praying for and offering the newly baptized person to God. "If this were done, nothing essential would be omitted; and that one ceremony, which came from God its author, not buried in outlandish pollutions, would shine in its full brightness."

With the same clarity and intensity, Calvin addressed all the major teachings of the Christian faith. Like the trained lawyer he was, Calvin lunged into the layers of tradition that, he believed, separated the Catholic Church of his day from the actual teachings of the Scriptures. Like the other reformers, Calvin wanted to reassert the Scriptures as the ultimate authority for the church and the Christian faith. All those years of study, of reading and writing in Latin, his firm grasp on the original languages of the Bible, and his readings in the early church fathers, came into focus as he set down his brilliant manifesto of Christianity. But this was only the beginning. He would rewrite and expand this book with new editions for the rest of his life.

Calvin estimated that the book, which was divided into six chapters, took him about eight months to write. He was certainly aware that he was not writing something brand-new. Calvin leaned heavily on the recently rediscovered writings of the early church fathers as well as those of his fellow reformers, such as Luther. But it was uniquely Calvin. As one of Calvin's biographers wrote, "There was a spiritual power behind his pen."

The *Institutes* expressed the essence of Christianity in a way that many people could grasp. Deeply impressed, Calvin's friend Olivétan predicted that it would become "a little handbook of Christ's church." He was right about that: the first version was a kind of handbook. The final version, though, would be much grander. Systematically laid out, it would become Calvin's bible about the Bible, maintaining its power to inspire and instruct through the centuries until today.

## A LETTER TO THE KING

One of the most striking features of this first edition was Calvin's open letter to the French king. Explaining his reasons for writing the book, Calvin began with a "Prefatory Address to King Francis." It is a masterpiece of persuasive writing. Calvin's language was respectful and diplomatic, yet pulled no punches. Still stung by the death of de la Forge and others, he wanted the monarch to reconsider his persecution of Protestants. It was a forceful plea for the king's clemency for himself and for his fellow Protestant believers.

We don't know whether Calvin really believed that the king would read his words and change his approach to allow room in France for these new ideas; it is quite likely that the king never read it. But perhaps Calvin's real purpose was to set before the whole world the worthiness of his cause.

In the letter, Calvin, the highly trained lawyer, lays out his case before "the Most mighty and illustrious monarch, Francis, Most Christian King of the French." He begins graciously, trying not to arouse the king's enmity. He's not trying to persuade the king of the truth of this new movement, he simply wants his king to be just in his dealings. He forcefully points out that people slander Protestants, giving the king the wrong idea of the true aims of this reform movement. He challenges the king for persecuting the new believers. "It is sheer violence that bloody sentences are meted out against a doctrine without a hearing." Standing in the lawyer's dock, Calvin argues his case for the Reformation, asking the king to reconsider his position: "For this reason, most invincible King, I not unjustly ask you to undertake a full inquiry into this case, which until now has been handled—we may even say, tossed about—with no order of law and with violent heat rather than judicial gravity."

In asking the king to look more deeply into the situation, Calvin argues that the reformers have not created a new religion at all. Gossips and liars attending the king's court, Calvin says, have unfairly stated that the reformers are trying to bring the church back to a pristine state that never really existed. He refutes the notion that these rebel believers, enthralled by the novelty of a new approach to faith, wanted to tear down a solid institution with an illustrious past and replace it with a stripped-down and heretical version of the faith: "First, by calling it 'new' they do great wrong to God, whose Sacred Word does not deserve to be accused of novelty." Characteristically, Calvin can't resist a note of sarcasm. "Indeed," he writes, "I do not at all doubt that it is new to them, since to them both Christ himself and his gospel are new."

Calvin goes on to argue that the reformers are teaching the very same things that were taught by the early church fathers. In reality, he says, it is the Catholic Church and its theologians who misconstrue what the early fathers, such as Jerome and Augustine, taught and preached. "The good things that these fathers have written they either do not notice, or misrepresent or pervert. You might say that their only care is to gather dung among gold." Calvin also argues that his enemies are misquoting church fathers for their own purposes. They misread and misjudge and teach an improper understanding of what they preached. And even when they get it right, they get it wrong: "If our opponents want to preserve the limits set by the fathers according to their understanding of them, why do they themselves transgress them so willfully as it suits them?"

Calvin then addresses the issue of custom or tradition and how they can subvert the truth of Scripture. Once again he criticizes the church in Rome for its empty rituals and its emphasis on appearance over substance. The Protestants, he says, object to practices that have little meaning to them. "To constrain us to yield to custom would be to treat us most unjustly." The real church is described in the Bible. It is a church that points to God's magnificence as well as to the grandeur of God's creation. Yet, it is also a church whose faith is, in essence, unseen. It cannot be captured in human-made images or expressed in the elaborate liturgies of the Catholic Church.

Bringing his case to a close, Calvin acknowledges that "this preface has grown almost to the bulk of a full apology. My object, however, was not to frame a defense, but only with a view to the hearing of our cause, to mollify your mind, now indeed turned away and estranged from us—I add, even inflamed against us—but whose good will, we are confident, we should regain, would you but once, with calmness and composure, read this our Confession, which we desire your Majesty to accept instead of a defense."

But if the "whispers of the malevolent" so possess the king's attention, telling and feeding him lies, and the king will not open his mind to new ideas, then perhaps no resolution can come. If in the end, the king fails to understand the Protestants' cause, and if they have no real chance to state their case, then, writes Calvin, "we will be reduced to the last extremity even as sheep destined for the slaughter."

God will be the final judge, notes Calvin, and therefore he and his fellow reformers will be patient, because "in our patience, we will possess our souls." They can be patient precisely because they also "await the strong hand of the Lord, which will surely appear in due season, coming forth armed to deliver the poor from their affliction and also to punish their despisers, who now exult with such great assurance." God, in other words, would eventually unsheathe a sword to cut down the persecutors. God would shed the mantle of peace and patience and punish those who had been killing his people.

Finally, reminding the king that he too was answerable to God, Calvin closes with the humility of a subject of God and the king. "Most illustrious King, may the Lord, the King of kings, establish your throne in righteousness, and your sceptre in equity."

After spending fifteen months working on the book and studying Hebrew, Calvin sent off his book to the publisher in Basel, wondering, perhaps, how the king might react to his opening statements.

## PREACHING TO A PRINCESS

His work on the *Institutes* completed, Calvin was ready for a change. In the spring of 1536 he traveled over the Alps to Italy. This trip wasn't just a vacation—it had a serious purpose as well. Calvin wanted to bring Christ to a princess.

Aware of dangers involved in his travel through Catholic territory, for this journey Calvin changed his name to Charles d'Espeville. His friend du Tillet joined him, taking on the name Louis de Haulmont. Their destination was Ferrera, in northern Italy, south of Venice—the royal court of princess Renee of France, daughter of King Louis XII. In many ways Renee was walking a delicate tightrope, trying to learn more about this new approach to faith while at the same time remaining ostensibly Catholic. She was a cousin of Marguerite d'Angoulême, the king's sister with whom Calvin had previously had contact, and who was also sympathetic to the reformers. Both women ended up being strong protectors of the reformers. But they suffered too, and Calvin stood by them as best he could until the end.

The reasons for this arduous and dangerous trip are not entirely clear, but it quite possible that they had been invited. In his biography, Beza says that Calvin wanted to pay his respects to Renee, "whose piety was at that time very much praised."

Once Calvin arrived, Renee wanted to hear more about the faith. Dressed as a nobleman, Calvin played it coy. He didn't want to draw attention to himself and his friend in the royal court. But he did have the opportunity to speak directly with the princess. "She was struck with Calvin's fine genius," says one historian. Aware of the dangers involved, Renee passed Calvin and du Tillet off as two men of letters who had come to visit Italy.

Over the years, this trip has been encrusted with legend. The biggest one is that Calvin was unmasked, arrested, and sent to Spain to be questioned by those who were running the Spanish Inquisition. Supposedly someone, at Renee's urging, came to his rescue and he escaped. But there is little historical record of this.

We do know that Calvin was impressed with Renee, whose court was a haven for those fleeing persecution in France. Calvin may even have had hopes of gaining favor in her court, perhaps finding there a safe place to stay along with a stipend to continue his writing. There is evidence that he did obtain employment for a time as one of Renee's secretaries. Apparently, though, it was hard for Calvin to find out just which way Renee leaned. Although she seemed to be profoundly attracted to the new ideas, she did not express clear agreement with them. She also had a soft spot in her heart for French refugees. Nonetheless, like most royal courts, this was a place of intrigue and many conflicting loyalties. It was hard to know whom to trust.

In any case, Calvin and Renee forged a bond of mutual respect, becoming lifelong correspondents. In his letters to Renee, Calvin spoke directly to her heart: "The main point is that the holy doctrine of our master should so transform us in mind and heart, that his glory may shine forth in us by innocence, integrity and holiness." He also highlighted his strong objections to the Catholic Church and its many superstitions, seeking to keep her committed to the cause. He exhorted her to never give up on the faith.

Beza wrote that Renee loved and honored Calvin for as long as he lived "as an excellent instrument of the Lord." He spoke several times to Calvin about Renee and her quest for faith. She was, says Beza, one of the women whose souls Calvin wished sincerely to save. In fact, Calvin instilled in her such a "sincere zeal for religion . . . that she continued ever after to entertain a sincere affection for him during his life, and now also as his survivor, exhibits striking marks of her gratitude after his death."

There is some evidence that Calvin may have actually preached and taught in a small chapel Renee had built. He found people interested in his views and willing to listen. Renee was pleased by what Calvin and others had to say. A new world seemed to be opening up, and she wanted to be part of it. She had glimpsed a Renaissance of ideas and art and social customs, and now she was seeing a new flowering of faith. It was a heady but frightening time to be a woman seeking change. Of Calvin and the others, she wrote: "They are of my nation, and if God had given me a beard on my chin, and I were a man, they would all be my subjects."

In the spring of 1536, Renee's court sheltered not only Calvin but also the Protestant poet—and later a writer of psalm texts for singing in churches— Clément Marot. He was among those suspected as masterminding the infamous Night of Placards back in Paris, the event that brought down the wrath of the king. Catholic authorities in Ferrera apparently got wind that he was in town, but they held off doing anything until one of Marot's friends, also suspected of being in on the Placards, caught their attention. This friend was a young singer known as Jehannet. Like Marot, he was an enemy of the empty, even blasphemous rituals of the Church of Rome.

On Good Friday, April 14, 1536, a service was held that drew people from Renee's court. The liturgy was somber and yet full of drama and pageantry. Worshipers reenacted the way of the cross, praying as they went from station to station along the road to Golgatha. A great litany of remorse was read. People were asked to put themselves in the place of Christ, who had been scourged and spat upon and degraded. At one point, the worshipers were asked to adore the cross. Lining up in the aisles, they moved forward slowly and, when they reached the front, bent to kiss the bloody feet of Christ affixed to the cross.

At some point during the service, Jehannet, the singer, decided that he had had enough. He stood and made quite a show of walking out before the lengthy service was over. His displeasure was so obvious and his flight from the sanctuary so unexpected that it drew a great deal of attention.

People were upset by what he had done. Many agreed that he had to be punished. Arrested and questioned by torture, the singer broke down. He listed for the authorities many of Renee's protégés and friends who had gathered around her to discuss the new views. Word circulated quickly of what the singer had told authorities. Most of those implicated, including Calvin and du Tillet, fled.

Calvin and du Tillet made their way back to Basel. Little did Calvin know at the time of the inner anguish his good friend was feeling. For a long time, du Tillet had been struggling over whether he ought to make a formal break with the Catholic Church. Du Tillet felt great affection for Calvin and spent countless hours talking and listening to him about the new approach to faith. But apparently he never really told Calvin of the deep conflict that he felt. He couldn't shake the tug of the Catholic Church and its rituals and beliefs, its long history and tradition. Many of his own family members were also well-known and respected Catholics. Yet he found the simplicity of love for Christ and belief in the Bible that Calvin taught attractive as well.

We can imagine him wondering, as they recrossed the Alps, if he ought to share his concerns with his friend. When he finally learned from his friend what was in his heart, Calvin wrote him a letter expressing his confusion and surprise: "I cannot conceal from you that I have been very much astonished on hearing of your intention, and even the reasons which are put forth along with the declaration of it in your letters. . . . What occasions the greatest surprise is that I considered you so settled and resolved in that affair."

# Chapter 5

# CALLED TO GENEVA

———

After a time Calvin went back to France to take care of family business. The king had granted a six-month period for heretics to return and then rejoin the Catholic Church. Some scholars say he went to Noyon at this time, and that this was when he learned that his older brother, Charles, had been executed by authorities as a heretic. More likely he stayed in Paris. Records show that on June 2, 1536, he gave power of attorney to his brother Antoine to sell the lands that had belonged to his parents. With the death of Charles, John became the legal guardian of the family's trust, such as it was. But he really didn't have the time or inclination to handle it properly.

Once the land transaction was complete, Antoine and their half-sister, Marie, joined John. They decided that in Strasbourg, where the Reformation had taken hold, they could begin a new life in safety. They began the trip, perhaps with a few other residents from Noyon in a caravan. Their spirits were troubled and yet they were also filled with hope because they were leaving France just as persecutions were beginning to occur again against reformers. The travellers took the most reasonable route, due east a few miles to Strasbourg, little knowing that they were headed toward a battlefield.

On July 25, 1536, the French army had crossed the border into Saxony as part of a larger struggle for power between the Holy Roman Emperor Charles V and French King Francis I. A general named Montmorency, to whom Francis entrusted the chief command, marched into the area with orders to devastate the countryside. Homes were razed. Crops burned. People killed. Roadblocks were put up. Fighting raged.

# ONE NIGHT IN GENEVA

It is not clear at what point Calvin and his entourage found out that a war was separating them from their destination. Taking a detour, they decided to stay one night in Geneva before pressing on. On that night, Calvin's life, and the direction of the Reformation, would forever be changed. Looking back, we see God's hand at work.

Calvin saw himself primarily as a man of letters. His *Institutes* were starting to make a name for him as an articulate defender of the Protestant faith. That night in Geneva, Calvin was ready to hunker down and get some sleep before heading out to Strasbourg early in the morning. He was not prepared for what would happen.

Somehow, a minister named Guillaume Farel heard that Calvin was in town. A large, red-bearded, blustery man, Farel had failed in 1532 in a first attempt at reformation in Geneva. He returned in 1533, this time under the protection of Berne, a nearby city under whose control Geneva had fallen. As a result of this change in Geneva's political situation, its reluctant citizens were persuaded by Berne to accept the teachings of the Reformation. Most were deeply entrenched in their Catholic identity, even if they weren't always pleased with how the Catholics had been running the city in the recent years.

But whatever ties Genevans had to the Church in Rome, the people must not have been all that committed, since they didn't put up much of a fight when a purge of all things Catholic began. In the summer of 1535, Farel seized the church of La Madeleine and the Cathedral of St. Pierre. The floodgates of change had been opened. This was just the opportunity Farel had been waiting for: "I have been baptized in the Name of the Father, the Son and the Holy Spirit. I go about preaching Christ, why He died for our sins and rose again for our justification. Whoever believes in Him will be saved; unbelievers will be lost." He and his followers went on a rampage—overturning votive candle stands, destroying statues, and tearing the altar drapes. They tore down crosses and ripped up pews, dismantled confessionals, and defaced stained glass windows portraying saints.

While this ecclesiastical vandalism is hard for us to understand today, it indicates the depth of hostility many of the reformers felt toward the idolatrous trappings of the church of that day. But Farel may have been a just a little too eager to step in and wipe out the vestiges of the past. Although he loved Christ and wanted to preach Christ, powerful emotions often got the best of him. In the heat of these emotions, he readily defaced and damaged the churches. Once word got around of how much damage he and his followers had done, people in Geneva grew angry. Some threatened him harm. In the backlash, he realized that if the reforms were to truly take hold in Geneva, they needed to be brought by someone who was less hotheaded than he. He also knew that Geneva was in danger of being reconquered by the Duke of Savoy on behalf of the Catholic Church. If that happened, all his hopes for the future would be squelched. He knew it was time to enlist the help of a man whose reputation was on the rise, and who was not known for being rash.

Farel rushed over to the place where Calvin was staying. He pounded on the door and barged into the room. Thus rudely awakened, weary from the road, and wanting simply to sleep before pushing on to Strasbourg, Calvin's first impression of Farel was of a madman. But as Farel paced back and forth in the room, spouting words of venom against the Catholic Church and pleading with Calvin to stay and help him create order out of the chaos of Geneva, Calvin began to see that this was someone "who burned with extraordinary zeal to advance the gospel." Even so, Calvin told him that he couldn't stay. When Farel had finally calmed down, Calvin told him that his calling was to be a writer, and he was headed to Strasbourg to do just that. He wished, he said, to keep himself "free from other pursuits." Farel, however, wasn't buying it. Getting up, Farel unfurled himself to his full, frightening height. He proceeded, says Calvin, "to utter the imprecation that God would curse my retirement and tranquility of studies which I sought, if I should withdraw and refuse to help, when the necessity was so urgent."

These words cut to the quick, reminding Calvin that his life was not his own. Try as he might to discount it, this thunderstorm of a man was speaking the truth. Calvin grew certain, although he hated this certainty, that God was speaking through Farel that night. "I was so terror-struck, that I gave up the journey I had undertaken."

That night Calvin came to accept that he would work with Farel in Geneva.

## THE WORK BEGINS

But the work in Geneva didn't begin right away. Calvin had some personal business to attend to in Basel, perhaps to gather some of his belongings and to check on the status of his book, which was becoming a bestseller. People had apparently been hungering for a clear description of this new approach to faith. Calvin's *Institutes* gave it to them in a language they could understand and a logic that held them in its grasp.

When he returned to Geneva, Calvin came down with a debilitating illness that put him in bed for a spell. Farel, however, was willing to wait for the young author and reformer to regain a modicum of health. Calvin battled sickness for much of his life, and this time he had been afflicted with a very painful infection of his gums. By the end of September 1536, Calvin dragged himself from his sick bed and pronounced himself fit enough to begin his ministry in Geneva. The town, he knew, remained in a precarious position politically. Morally it was in profound need of pastoral attention and leadership. Soldiers from Berne, who had helped wrest Geneva from the control of the Catholics, still patrolled the streets. Calvin was inaugurated into the ministry there with no pomp and circumstance, no ordination with the laying of hands. It appears that Farel simply told him that his first task would be to teach the Epistles of Paul to people who gathered for instruction in the St. Pierre Cathedral, which had been stripped of its Catholic trappings. Calvin was given the title of Professor of Sacred Letters in the Church of Geneva.

But before Calvin could begin expounding on the letters of St. Paul, Farel spirited him off eastward around Lake Geneva, a picturesque body of water surrounded by mountains, to the town of Lausanne. Along the way, Farel told Calvin that they were headed to Lausanne to take part in a public debate sponsored by the officials in Berne on the merits of Lausanne becoming a Protestant city. At this point, communities had two choices—to remain Catholic or make the break to Protestantism. Calvin and Farel arrived as townspeople gathered and farmers flowed in from the countryside to hear both sides of the discussion before casting ballots on which approach to embrace. On October 1, beating drums announced the start of the debate. Deputies from Berne wearing black doublets, red hose, and wide-brimmed, feathered hats sat on fancy chairs, prepared to hear both sides of the argument. Secretaries had their quills ready to record the debate.

As Farel and others debated Catholic representatives in the festive, open air, Calvin sat silent, still nursing his gum disease and a cold. He didn't want to be there, and he certainly hadn't planned to join in the debate. But at some point one of the Catholic representatives began talking about how the Protestants really missed the point on what the church fathers for centuries past had been teaching about the Lord's Supper: that the actual body and blood of Christ resided in the bread and the wine. Having dealt with this topic in his new book, Calvin now felt compelled to speak on this crucial point. He rose angrily from his seat to refute the Catholic speaker on point after point, frequently quoting from memory actual words and arguments of the church fathers. We can imagine Farel watching and listening to the young theologian with great satisfaction. *This* was why Farel had urged Calvin to get his hands dirty in the real work of the church, instead of simply writing about it from a distance. Calvin's arguments persuaded many, and at the end of the day the town voted to become Protestant. Perhaps Farel pounded his skinny partner on the back in triumph on the way home. Likely, both men were happy and yet apprehensive as they made their way back to Geneva, where the hard work had yet to begin.

Located almost directly on the way from Italy to France and settled in the midst of the warring Swiss provinces, Geneva was a walled and fortified town of more than 10,000 people, known for their independent mindset. Although they had voted to be Protestant, few people had any idea what this new faith taught—they were more or less hoping it simply meant fewer intrusions by the Catholic Church and more freedom for themselves. The Mass was gone, monasteries were closed, and papal authority renounced, leaving them to formulate a new way forward. That way would be easy—or so they hoped. Calvin decided it was his duty to help them realize just how wrong they were. Soon after returning from Lausanne, he decided to draw up a set of rules with explanations to guide this new way forward.

Calvin wrote quickly and in earnest, drawing from much of what he had already written in *The Institutes*. He detailed specific rules and regulations and ways by which Genevans could live by the code laid down by God in the Bible. Calvin's vision was for Geneva to become a holy city, an example of how a municipality could arrange itself for the spiritual benefit of its people. He hoped to put into practice laws that would make Geneva become a city of God. With Farel urging him on, Calvin drafted a memorandum titled "Articles on the Ruling of the Church." Beza describes it as a "formulary of doctrine suited to the state of the church in Geneva, which was only just emerging from the corruptions of popery."

The articles were divided into four parts, and at first seemed workable to the town fathers. The first article, though, proved to be contentious, once made into law. It called for only worthy people to be given the right to participate in the Lord's Supper. Who was to determine the worthiness of Genevans to participate? According to Calvin, preachers and their designates, a group of pious men in various quarters of the city, were given this charge. Their task, in part, was to observe their neighbors, making sure that everyone in their area of influence lived a godly life. A godly life, it seemed, mostly had to do with not violating the virtues set down in the Bible. Drunkenness, infidelity, lying, cheating, stealing, and a few other behaviors were among those that could require a sinner to appear before a minister to repent of his or her wrongdoings. If people failed to ask for forgiveness and promise to mend their ways, the ministers would have the power to excommunicate wrongdoers from the church, denying them access to the Lord's Supper. Even then, publicly repenting of their sin would allow them back into the good graces of the church and able to partake of Communion. The issue here was ultimate authority—who had the right to excommunicate? Only the preachers, or members of the city council as well? In other words, who was really in charge of the morals of the city? This issue would continue to dog Calvin throughout his entire stay in Geneva.

In the articles, Calvin wrote succinctly about the Lord's Supper and why the clergy ought to have the power of excommunication. "The principal rule that is required, and for which it is necessary to have the greatest care, is that this Holy Supper, ordained and instituted for joining members of our Lord Jesus Christ with their Head and with one another in one body and one spirit, be not soiled and contaminated by those coming to it and communicating, who declare and manifest by their misconduct and evil life that they do not at all belong to Jesus." These are harsh words, but they tell us how important the Lord's Supper was to Calvin and the significant central role it played in the life of a believer. Some saw him as an angry demagogue or as an unflinching purist. The second charge, at least, he would have proudly accepted.

Other parts of the articles were less controversial. One called for psalms to be sung during services, a practice also growing elsewhere in Protestant churches. Bringing song into the church was a breath of fresh air that many people embraced. It made people in the pews participants, not simply spectators in the worship of God. Guidelines for marriage and teaching the children the basics of the faith in a catechism were also part of the articles Calvin crafted. The catechism was in many ways a condensed version of *The Institutes*, which Calvin continued to rewrite. As it turned out, the catechism was way over the heads of the youth.

In part, Calvin's articles fit with ideas proposed and discussed centuries before by Augustine, one of the church fathers whose works Calvin had read faithfully. Augustine called for an earthly city of God. The city that someday would rise from the ruins of Rome, argued Augustine, "must be based upon Christian principles. Warfare, economic activity, education, and the rearing of children should all be conducted in a Christian spirit."

Calvin was deeply moved by this vision and tried to employ it right from the start in Geneva. Humans were by nature sinful and evil, greedy and grasping for their own pleasure, Calvin believed. It was the job of the church, hand in hand with the state, to repress and restrain and, when necessary, punish people in order to keep them in the Christian life as laid out in the Bible.

In order to understand Calvin's struggle in the years to come, it's important to grasp the political scene in Geneva at this time. The magistrates in charge of the government were called *syndics*. There were four of them, elected annually by a designated assembly of men. The syndics were in charge of the *Little Council*, which was made up of twenty-five members who met to take care of the city's civil and foreign business at least three times a week. This was the city's main administrative body. In addition, the *Council of Two Hundred* met monthly to review important matters. For the purposes of this book, these people will be collectively referred to as "lawmakers" or "city officials." The key fact is that the Little Council, in many ways, held the power and effectively passed it on from year to year.

It was this council, for instance, that first reviewed the articles Calvin and Farel presented early in 1537. Sensing the need to fill the void left following the removal of Roman authority, the council considered the articles and fairly quickly enacted them into law. But, as we've already noted, the first article caused an uproar. People didn't like the idea of someone checking up on them and then reporting back to some religious authority. Although this wasn't an entirely new concept, Calvin's articles offered a twist: he wanted the church, not the state, to have control over people's behavior by maintaining the right of excommunication.

While some decried Calvin's call to enlist a small force of like-minded believers to monitor citizens' morals, it's important to note that he did not do this out of spite or from a personal desire for power. As he explained in the 1538 Preface to the Genevan Catechism, his intent was pastoral. He wanted pastors to be guides for good and wholesome living and to help people avoid sin. Pastors, especially, were to follow the rules well. As those held responsible for their flock, they were to serve as role models, counselors, teachers, and, of course, preachers. This was not morality by consensus but rather disciplined, faithful living, for good purpose. "Whatever others may think," wrote Calvin, "we certainly do not regard our office as bound in so narrow limits that when the sermon is delivered we may rest as if our task were done. They whose blood will be required of us, if lost through our slothfulness, are to be cared for much more closely and vigilantly." In other words, practice what you preach. Calvin meant this, and he lived it.

Another point of contention that arose in the midst of the conflict over excommunication was that Calvin and Farel wanted the council to pass a requirement that everyone make a public profession of faith. The call for this type of allegiance was seen by some as yet another intrusion on their privacy, if not an assault to their conscience. On this issue, the lawmakers balked. In spite of these issues, for the good of the city, the city fathers passed the articles.

# POLITICAL MANEUVERING

But the articles had hardly been passed when, seemingly out of nowhere, charges were leveled at Farel and Calvin as heretics who didn't believe in the teaching of the Trinity. A few years hence, Calvin would struggle with this issue again in a case involving a man named Servetus, who was notorious for his rejection of the Trinity. Calvin and Farel were, of course, staunch believers of the Trinity, although Farel's writing on the subject had been less than fully clear. Apparently this lack of clarity was enough to cause trouble for both men.

Suspicions ran rampant during this hectic period, with some imagining heretics lurking around every corner. The man accusing Calvin and Farel was Pierre Caroli, a would-be reformer who also had the reputation of being something of a loose cannon. A vain and quarrelsome man, he shifted from one place to another but finally ended up back in the Catholic Church in Rome.

Furious over what he saw as trumped-up charges, Calvin had to travel to Berne to defend himself. Rising passionately to the occasion, Calvin pointed out the ways in which he taught the Trinity in all his writings. He spoke about praying for the dead as well, another of Caroli's charges, detailing and defending his beliefs. Although Calvin made a good impression, the government commissioners in Berne weren't quite sure what to think. They asked more questions, which Calvin answered with patience and intelligence. Once Calvin had made his case, the commissioners exonerated him and said he could leave, once again in their good graces. Farel, on the other hand, needed to answer more questions and explain some of the things he had written, or failed to write, about the Trinity. When he heard this, Calvin refused to separate himself from the case. He was with Farel, and the commissioners would have to decide: either declare them both orthodox or brand them heretics. The commissioners put things off until May, when there was another debate involving some highly technical teachings about prayers for the dead that, five hundred years later, no longer seem compelling. Once again, Calvin the lawyer argued his case with great precision and emotion. (Meanwhile, Farel was doing some behind-the-scenes persuasion by telling a few key people about Caroli's loose morals.) By June 1, 1537, the commissioners exonerated both Calvin and Farel of the charges. They determined that Caroli was the real problem. And as they turned their attention on Caroli, Calvin and Farel went back to Geneva.

Problems, though, were not over for Calvin and Farel. Returning to Geneva, they learned that a couple of Anabaptists from the Netherlands had appeared before city authorities. These men wanted the city to look more deeply into how Calvin and Farel and others were interpreting the Bible. Once again Calvin sprang into action, explaining why he did not like Anabaptist teachings. In the end, the Anabaptists failed to impress the city fathers and, after some discussion, the commissioners sent them on their way. With this victory, Calvin probably hoped things would finally settle down and he could go about his real job of teaching and preaching the gospel.

Many of Geneva's citizens were still very unhappy about what they saw as the clergy acting as neighborhood spies. They had voted for this Protestant religion, of course, but they certainly hadn't expected it to lead to neighbors checking up on neighbors and sinners having to go before ministers for examination. Calvin soon became the focus of the people's wrath—after all, he had written the articles. The townsfolk started complaining and blaming Calvin for being a killjoy and a demagogue. Matters got to the point that some people wrote nasty ballads against Calvin; someone even offered money to hire a hit man to kill Calvin.

Through all the political maneuvering Calvin and Farel stood fast, demanding that the city enforce the articles as written. This was an unhappy and tumultuous time for Calvin. He was, after all, still a relatively young man who was inexperienced in the role of pastor. Had he developed better political instincts, a bad situation might have been avoided. While a chorus of criticism seemed to greet him on every street corner, Calvin at first gently admonished people to follow the articles. But as the people became more hardheaded, so too did Calvin.

As the situation dragged on, a change started to come over Calvin. Increasingly, he saw himself as a prophet, as God's instrument in a depraved world. His hackles started to rise. The reasonable and retiring Calvin of his earlier years was gradually changing into a person who seemed to have less acceptance for ideas other than his own. Perhaps so much criticism had fouled his mood. Maybe the myriad of physical ills that he was continuing to experience, exacerbated by the constant need to defend himself, caused him to be less tolerant than he knew he should be. Whatever the case, he began fighting back.

Having been duly elected and named a preacher in Geneva, Calvin stood in the high pulpit of St. Pierre and began to wag his finger at the people, loudly denouncing those who threw dice, played cards, danced, drank too much, or visited prostitutes. He told the people that he wanted to see them at the Lord's Table, but only if they prepared for it and were worthy of the sacrament. People found themselves chastised and challenged by these fiery sermons. For some this was a welcome circumstance; others didn't like it at all. They started to see religion as an obstacle to fun rather than a path to salvation. Across the city a movement stirred as people chafed under the vehemence Calvin brought to the pulpit and began to question the value of this new faith.

But Calvin didn't just rant about the need to prepare for the Lord's Supper. He also preached against men who abused their wives and spoke about the need for children to be taught the true path to good living and faithful worship from the very beginning. In addition, he had a hand in helping to bring a welfare system to Geneva. He believed that he was called by God to make life better for the people, especially the poor. In 1535, officials in Geneva opened a hospital for the poor in a former convent. The church helped pay for the staff and for the care of patients, and a board of men from the church met regularly to talk about issues facing the hospital.

During this time, Calvin made a plea to his long-time traveling companion, Louis du Tillet, to come to Geneva to help him to try to stabilize the turbulent situation. Although du Tillet had returned to the Catholic Church and declined to come, he offered to lend his friend some money, since Calvin was living on a pauper's salary during those early years in Geneva. As much as he could have used the money, Calvin refused. He felt that his friend had turned against him by returning to Catholicism. In fact, he saw it as a bribe, a way for du Tillet to absolve himself from his decision and to maintain ties to his friend. Prior to this incident, Calvin had been kind to his friend. But in a series of letters that flowed between them throughout 1538, Calvin's tone became less and less accepting, and finally the correspondence ended. Calvin could no longer stomach writing his former friend, who in his letters kept challenging Calvin to think hard about his faith and especially his approach to ministry.

Busy as he was with the politics of building the church in Geneva, Calvin did not neglect his pastoral duties. He visited the sick and helped those in need however he could. When he learned sometime in the late 1530s that one of Farel's family members had been brought to Basel, suffering from the plague, Calvin, who was himself sick, rushed to the bedside of the family member. He waited as the man's illness grew dire. Sitting with the sick man, Calvin prayed fervently, and as the man's condition worsened, prepared him for death. When the man died, Calvin, poor as he was, dug into his pockets and paid for the burial.

But Calvin's positions and his firm stance on the pulpit ensured that he would always be tangled in the swirling politics of the city. The battles never seemed to end, particularly over the article giving the church in Geneva the power of excommunication. People never stopped complaining, and eventually the intensity of their anger forced the Genevan council to back off. The magistrates told the preachers that, though they would enforce the articles that they passed, the ministers could not refuse the Lord's Supper to anyone. Calvin was understandably upset over this amendment to a key aspect of the reform program he had drawn up. He felt betrayed and his anger began to boil, setting the stage for an eventual showdown.

## BANISHED

Tough as the fight was to establish a new order in Geneva, the job got even harder after the annual elections of 1538, which brought to power opponents of the changes that Farel and Calvin wanted. The results seemed to unleash a pent-up fury by a faction that Calvin dubbed the Libertines. When they passed Calvin or Farel on the streets, the Libertines would hurl insults and threaten violence. It's hard to imagine what these confrontations did to Calvin. By now he had become ever more convinced that he was God's mouthpiece and so he fought these attacks back with words, often spoken at the top of his lungs. Things deteriorated to the point that city officials had to step in and tell critics to back off and leave

Calvin and Farel to their business. At this point one might assume that Calvin would have backed off as well. But he didn't. In fact, he renewed his call that everyone should make a public confession of faith. He was so persuasive that city officials called for all Protestants to appear in church and announce their belief in this new faith. Many people complied, if begrudgingly, while others refused to do so.

With the new council in power, Calvin, Farel, and Corault, another local minister, began to lose what influence that they had. As one controversy followed another and people grew more recalcitrant, Corault, who was deeply respected by Calvin and Farel, took to the pulpit and denounced the people in the city, especially the Libertines on the council, for veering from the proper course—even calling them names. Infuriated, some people reported Corault to the authorities, who acted quickly. They ordered Corault to keep to the biblical texts when preaching and to leave politics and personal resentments at the door. Calvin and Farel saw this as an attempt to muzzle all preachers. They made it abundantly clear that they would not hold back when they were preaching the Word of God. Regardless of laws that had been passed or edicts laid down, the ministers told lawmakers that they worked for the Lord—not for the city of Geneva.

Ill will grew and people on all sides dug in. On November 26, 1538, the two ministers appeared before lawmakers and again demanded that it enforce the requirement that everyone in town subscribe publicly to the Protestant faith. But as more and more people were refusing to do so by this point, the ministers' demand fell, for the most part, on deaf ears. Calvin sensed that the reformers' position was becoming a lost cause. Whatever influence they had held only a year before had nearly vanished. Even so, the ministers had no intention of going out without a fight. They simply waited and bided their time.

Then came the final blow. Officials in Geneva, upon hearing that Farel and Calvin planned to refuse Communion to those unwilling to publicly confess to the faith, enlisted the support of their fellow lawmakers in Berne. These men looked the situation over and wrote back to Geneva, determining that the ministers could, in fact, deny communion to whomever they deemed unfit to receive the sacrament. But there was a rub. Bernese officials said that the bread distributed at Communion must be unleavened, just as it was at the original Lord's Supper. In addition, these officials decided that the ministers in Geneva must restore the baptismal fonts that the reformers had taken out, having deemed them another sign of popery. They also required that Calvin, Farel, Corault, and the other ministers restore some of the religious festivals, such as Christmas. For the most part, Calvin held that festivals and church holidays were not biblical and took away from the focus of the church.

At this point, Corault took to his pulpit again and blasted the lawmakers. Soon after he climbed down from his lofty perch, city officials arrested him and threw him in jail. This drew loud protests from Farel and Calvin. When the council told Calvin and Farel that they would ease some of their restrictions if the two pastors agreed to bar Corault from ever preaching again, they stubbornly refused. Storming out of the council chambers, pushing their way through an angry, gathering mob, they returned to their respective churches.

Easter Sunday was coming up. Between them, Farel and Calvin decided to preach on that holiest of days, but not to distribute Communion if city officials insisted on the unleavened form of bread. From a distance, the controversy over unleavened bread seems slight, but it was a matter of significance to the two reformers. They were committed to a cause they deemed right. Even when a city official appeared at their door on the night before Easter, pleading with them to relent and use unleavened bread, they held fast. In truth, the issue of the bread was not all that important to Calvin. The real issue was that he refused to be told by civil officials how he could conduct a worship service. These struggles were making Calvin testier by the day, and his ability to accept views outside of his own was diminishing—perhaps the curse for all prophets.

On Easter both men preached in the morning and in the afternoon. The sanctuaries were packed with people who came to see if the pastors would indeed refuse to distribute Communion. We can imagine the people stirring in the church, looking at one another—some hoping the pastors would give in to stave off more trouble, others hoping the pastors would stand up for their beliefs. They didn't have long to find out. Communion was not distributed that Easter Sunday in Geneva.

Why was Calvin so stubborn? One answer is that Calvin tended to follow Farel's lead, and Farel almost always charged ahead. But there was also something deeper at work in the Easter communion incident and at many other times. Writing in the shelter of the study or library was one thing, but actually being a preacher with responsibilities to the church and to the community was different. For a long time Calvin had been writing about his overarching vision for how the church should relate to a city. But now he was in a position to enact it. He believed he was working for God, and he felt conscience-bound to live by the truth as he encountered it in the Bible. Some writers portray Calvin as driven by a mystic's sense of purpose and otherworldly transcendence. But he was also a practical thinker who linked in his writing and preaching what he felt with what he saw and believed. Answering to a higher power, Calvin was determined to follow what he believed God wanted of him. His refusal to bend was both his strength and his weakness.

After the Easter Sunday incident, city officials wasted no time in deciding what to do. They ordered the pastors who refused to give Communion to leave the city. Barely two years after beginning the work in Geneva, Calvin found himself banished. Although it must have hurt him, Calvin took it in stride. "Certainly, had I been in the service of men, this would have been a bad reward," he wrote. "But it is well that I have served Him, who never fails to repay his servants whatever he has once promised." Calvin and Farel planned to appeal their banishment. At the same time, Calvin took on some of the blame for doing a poor job as a pastor, and especially as a diplomat to city officials. "We may indeed acknowledge before God and his people that it is in some measure owing to our unskillfullness, indolence, negligence, and error that the Church committed to our care had fallen into such a sad state of collapse," he would later write.

# Chapter 6

# BANISHED!
# ON TO STRASBOURG

---

After being ousted, Calvin and Farel traveled first to Berne and then Zurich to protest their removal and to petition officials for reinstatement. Officials there sided with the preachers and asked Geneva to reconsider. But it soon became clear that the lawmakers in Geneva wanted to be rid of the two reformers, along with Corault, for good. They were in no mood to invite any of them back.

Next Calvin and Farel headed toward Basel, where they planned to rest and regroup. Torrential rains made crossing the Rhine River a dangerous journey—at one point they were swept up in the raging current and barely made it safely to the other side. Tired, wet, and battered by the river's force, they finally reached Basel in May 1538. At first, the two bachelors planned to stay together. Although they presented a common front, some people were telling Calvin that Farel was too hotheaded to work with on the daunting task of establishing the Protestant church in Geneva. Although Calvin defended his friend and refused to take the criticism seriously, Farel was soon called away to take charge of a church in Neuchâtel, a medieval town about eighty miles west of Basel. Farel had been there before to bring the teachings of the Reformation, and the people knew him and liked him. He spent the rest of his life serving as pastor of the church in Neuchâtel.

Meanwhile, Calvin was once again wondering whether his vocation really was to live the quiet life of a writer and scholar. He wondered if perhaps

Farel had *not* been speaking for God that night in Geneva when he burst into that room where Calvin and his brother were staying on their way to Strasbourg. Calvin had mixed feelings. Even though he believed he was working for God, he couldn't help but feel wounded by his eighteen months in Geneva. He knew his failure in Geneva was in part his fault, and he wondered if what God really wanted was for him to write in the quiet atmosphere of a study. So Calvin prepared to stay on in Basel and continue his life as a writer and scholar.

## AN INVITATION FROM BUCER

Once again, the hand of God intervened. The pastors of the nearby town of Strasbourg invited Calvin to serve as pastor to the many French people who were crossing the border and flooding into the town. At first Calvin refused. He wasn't ready to plunge back into the fulltime pastorate. He told himself that someone else was probably better suited for that job.

But Calvin wasn't allowed to slip gently back into the sedate career of a scholar. Among those working as a pastor in Strasbourg was Martin Bucer, one of the great reformers. He was considered by many as second only to Luther in Germany. Under Bucer's strong leadership and well-balanced personality, Strasbourg had embraced the Reformation. Bucer was gentle at first, simply inquiring if Calvin would like to come to Strasbourg. When Calvin balked, Bucer applied more pressure. And when Calvin still remained reluctant, Bucer worked on him just as Farel had worked on him in Geneva. He denounced Calvin for his unwillingness to serve in Strasbourg. He questioned whether Calvin was ready to refuse God's call back into the ministry. He even accused Calvin of being another Jonah, shirking his responsibility to heed God's call and serve God's people. He portrayed Calvin's desire for the life of a scholar as cringing in the belly of the whale. Finally Calvin relented, convinced that Bucer, for whom Calvin had great respect, may actually have had his best interests at heart.

Calvin went to Strasbourg and took over the five hundred-strong French-speaking congregation in the Church of St. Nicholas. Strasbourg at that time was German, and German was the main language. The refugees needed someone like Calvin to preach to them in their native tongue.

To Calvin's delight, he soon discovered that Strasbourg was thoroughly Reformed, having accepted the Reformation faith back in the 1520s, unlike Geneva, which became Protestant only because the people saw it as the lesser of two evils. Little did Calvin know when he started how much this place would feed his soul. Here, among like-minded French people, he breathed a sigh of relief. Almost from the start, the people in the congregation appreciated and respected him. At first, it seemed unreal, and Calvin trod gently, testing the personalities of the people who filled his church. But they seemed to truly accept and respect him. He was relieved to find no sign of the problems that had constantly confronted him in Geneva.

Calvin soon devoted himself entirely to his new work. He preached or lectured every day. In addition to preaching twice on Sunday at what he called the "little Church," Calvin found himself in and out of the people's homes, getting to know them as he offered pastoral care. Through this pastoral work, he found that the congregation seemed to be in tune with his ideas.

As he had wanted to do in Geneva, Calvin instituted the monthly celebration of the Lord's Supper. The people took to this readily, believing, as Calvin did, that this sacrament was crucial for their faith. From the pulpit, Calvin spoke to his flock about how every congregation should be a Eucharistic community. He saw the Lord's Supper as the sign and symbol of a connection to Jesus, and as such he believed that it should be held in the highest esteem by members of the congregation. Mirroring his work in Geneva, he took on the task of interviewing people before allowing them to take Communion. He did this in lieu of the Catholic confession, in which people came to priests for absolution for their sins. Calvin still believed that people should be held responsible for their acts, but he was under no illusion that he was in any position to forgive their sins. That power belonged only to God. Nonetheless, it is hard to escape the aspect of judgment connected with the Lord's Supper here, given that Calvin was deciding who could and who could not partake.

Following Bucer's lead, he also wrote a liturgy for worship, quite similar in its basic structure to the one used in many Reformed churches worldwide today. He had tried some of these elements while in Geneva, but there his efforts to introduce innovation were stymied by controversy. With the help of Bucer, Calvin developed a liturgy that made room for variables depending on the circumstances. Calvin was to follow this liturgy, with some adjustments, throughout his life.

## CALVIN'S LITURGY

Assembly
Opening sentences
Confession of sin
The Ten Commandments (sung)
Psalm (sung)
*Word*
Collect for Illumination
Lesson and Sermon
Prayer of Intercession
Apostles' Creed (sung)
*Meal*
The Lord's Supper
Prayer of Thanksgiving
Psalm (sung) or Canticle of Simeon (sung)
*Sending*
Offering for the poor
Blessing

During his time in Strasbourg, Calvin continued to revise this liturgy. He especially tried to focus on the specific context in which the French refugees found themselves. Experiment as he did, especially with singing, he remained opposed to the use of musical instruments, especially an organ, in worship, believing that these instruments took people's attention away from serious prayer and worship. It is important to underscore here Calvin's love of using the psalms in song. He wrote a few of these psalm songs himself. The human voice was a divinely created instrument, Calvin believed, and singing was the highest form of praise and worship. He was sure God delighted in hearing these songs sung before him.

The city of Strasbourg itself provided a welcome and surprising serenity for Calvin. With no mobs to harass him and no one putting a price on his head, Calvin was free to stroll the streets in peace. He walked along the river and contemplated the huge sandstone Gothic Roman Catholic Cathedral that dominated the town—famous throughout Europe for its clock that told the position of the planets as well as the time of day. Calvin delighted in hearing it ringing, and its celestial aspect always brought his mind back to God.

Calvin's church was near Bucer's home, and he stopped by often to chat with the older reformer, who was then in his sixties. Bucer became a mentor, perhaps one of the most influential that Calvin ever had. Calvin was attracted to his easy and graceful nature. Although Bucer was filled with ideas, he always made time to listen carefully to what Calvin had to say. Sitting together on a wooden bench in Bucer's busy home, they spoke of many things, especially about the work of Augustine. They shared books and talked about what they'd read. Bucer told him stories of his times working with Martin Luther. Respect and love flourished between the reformers. At the same time, there were disagreements, and Calvin didn't shy away from telling Bucer where he thought his theology was lacking. Yet Calvin learned a great deal from Bucer as well. Perhaps one of the most personal lessons he learned was the great joy that a man could take in his family. Bucer clearly cherished his wife and thought highly of his children and grandchildren, who were often underfoot or making demands on his time. Calvin saw in Bucer's home a mutual caring that his own home in Noyon had lacked.

At the same time, Calvin continued to face disappointments and grief. Soon after he began his pastorate at Strasbourg he grieved the death of Corault, his old friend from Geneva. He also learned of the death in Italy of his good friend Olivétan, the one who had first influenced him to think about the faith to which he ended up dedicating his life. This death too plunged Calvin into sadness and loss. During this period, he resumed writing to du Tillet, hoping to bring him back into the Protestant fold, an attempt that failed as du Tillet refused to reconsider. Maybe these losses, along with his ongoing health problems, contributed to Calvin's ongoing reputation for having a quick temper, which tended to erupt with little apparent provocation.

One such incident involved Pierre Caroli, the renegade who had accused Calvin and Farel of heresy back in Geneva. Without prior notice, he appeared on the scene, having left the Roman Church, apparently hoping to serve as a pastor in Strasbourg. Farel befriended and encouraged him. But Caroli couldn't resist once again accusing Calvin and Farel of opposing some of the ancient creeds—a trumped up charge to be sure. Since the Strasbourg officials wanted to be sure, this accusation led to an investigation. In the end, the authorities concluded that this was not heresy but a case of conflict between personalities. They took what they hoped would be the easiest way out for everyone involved: they wrote up a document of reconciliation, hoping everyone would sign it and then all move forward.

In this, the officials had seriously misjudged Calvin. When he saw this document, which implied that Farel and Calvin had erred in not signing on to three ancient creeds, Calvin exploded. This minute point had nothing to do with what Calvin or Farel thought or believed; it was yet another example of church politics gone awry. By trying to please everyone in their document of reconciliation, church officials only succeeded in drawing Calvin's wrath. Bucer delivered the paper, perhaps hoping for a quick resolution of the matter. Angrily Calvin flung the paper in the air, saying he would die before signing it, and rushed from the room. As he stood heaving and sputtering with righteous indignation, Calvin did not want to listen to reason. Eventually, Bucer was able to calm him down. The clause that had caused Calvin such trouble was dropped, and he signed it.

Calvin was well aware of his tendency toward anger. It was a shortcoming, he knew, and one he tried hard to hold at bay. He spoke of it often in his letters and even more frequently prayed to God to help rid him of this scourge. Recalling the Caroli incident in a letter to Farel, Calvin wrote, "the bile had taken entire possession of my mind, and I poured out bitterness on all sides. . . . When I got home, I was seized with an extraordinary paroxysm (of guilt), nor did I find any other solace than in sighs and tears."

With little income from the refugees' church or his writing, Calvin had to take in boarders and maybe even sell some of his books to make ends meet. This poverty did not discourage him—money never seemed all that important to Calvin. Ministry and writing and teaching were his passions. During the three years Calvin was in Strasbourg he was able to get a good deal of writing done. He wrote and published his famous *Commentary on Romans,* a book that was to serve as a model for many biblical commentaries that followed. It included a translation from the Greek and was followed by an exegesis and exposition of the text in Calvin's unusually clear and down-to-earth but polished prose. Calvin also published a second, considerably updated version of his *Institutes.* This great work of his life was by now doctrinally complete, but he would continue working on it in coming years.

## A REBUTTAL

Although Calvin had been banished from Geneva, he was still interested in what was going on there. He began to feel pangs of regret and wondered if anyone could ever turn that city around. Had he somehow failed the people of Geneva by his impetuousness? When it became clear to him that the citizens of Geneva had not by any means thrown off the yoke of their wayward ways, he took some of the blame on himself. Five months after leaving the city, and then again at nine months, he wrote letters encouraging people to remain strong in the faith he had taught them. He also counseled the people still attending St. Pierre Cathedral to work toward harmony—exactly what Christ would have wanted of them.

Then he learned of a letter that had been sent to Geneva in April 1539 by Cardinal James Sadoleto, bishop of Carpentras in France, in which the Catholic prelate tried to win back the favor of the Genevans to Rome. The letter did not specifically mention Calvin or Farel, but it seems clear that he saw a vacuum in their absence and wanted to woo people to the faith of their grandfathers. In his letter, says Beza, Sadoleto pulled out all of the stops, opening with gushing flattery and moving on to address the Genevan people as a concerned and benevolent father would address his children. They had lost their way, he wrote, and it was time for them to return home to the cradling comfort of the church that had always loved them. But the cardinal also used some tough talk, meant to prick their consciences. Their salvation, Sadoleto warned, was at stake unless they returned to the one true church. He appealed to the stability of the past, a time when Mother Church had overseen people's needs and led them on the righteous path to heaven. The church, he reminded them, traced its roots back to Christ. Its teachings and its trappings were an age-old means of connecting them more closely with God. The Catholic Church taught people to live holy, prayerful lives. In his letter, he writes two fictional speeches given by his adversaries—perhaps Calvin and Farel—exposing their "ambition, avarice, love of popular applause, inward fraud and malice."

When Calvin read the cardinal's letter and realized that no one in Geneva was up to the challenge of rebuttal, he poured himself into writing a 15,000-word response, goaded by the cardinal's arrogant tone and especially his presumption that, if given the chance, the people would willingly return to the Catholic Church. It took Calvin six frantic days to write his brilliant "Reply to Sadoleto." In it he marshaled all his theological learning and his training as a lawyer, taking on the cardinal point by point and countering each of his arguments. On the issue of justification by faith alone, an important part of the Protestant bulwark, Calvin insisted that works alone are "not worth one single straw." He also argued that the reformers were not, as Sadoleto charged, sinning against the early church fathers and trying to tear down the church for no good reason. Rather, he said, the reformers were returning to the true practices of the church as it evolved from Christ's commands in the early church, and waging war against "all the adulterers" who have been "laying snares for [the church's] chastity." Calvin's letter silenced Sadoleto and helped to increase his own prestige as an articulate and stalwart defender of the faith.

## CALVIN FINDS A WIFE

The relative serenity of his life in Strasbourg allowed Calvin to consider his own loneliness. Perhaps unsurprisingly, Calvin's was not a typical love story, full of wooing and accompanied by heart-rendering crescendos of music. John Calvin pursued a wife in a way that was unique to him— carefully, methodically, and with a view to what this would mean for the future. His mentor, the happily married Bucer, was the person who first nudged Calvin in this direction. Others, including the happy marriage of Pierre Viret, a fiery preacher and one of Calvin's longtime colleagues, may have influenced him as well, or at least opened his eyes and heart to the possibility of marriage. There were also practical, pastoral reasons for Calvin to find a wife. Protestants didn't believe in celibacy for their pastors, and it would be good, Bucer told him, if Calvin could serve as a role model in this area as well by taking a wife.

Giving the matter considerable thought, Calvin decided this might be a good idea, although his letters indicate his awareness that it might also be problematic. After all, he did suffer from gout, headaches, stomach ailments, hemorrhoids, and chronic asthma. And as for his bank account, it was next to nonexistent. In other words, Calvin realized that he wasn't exactly a major catch. At the same time, he had his standards: "I am none of those insane lovers who embrace also the vices of those they are in love with, when they are smitten at first sight with a fine figure," he wrote. "This only is the beauty which attracts me: if she is chaste, if not too nice or fastidious, if economical, if patient, if there is hope that she will be interested about my health."

Finally convinced that he ought to seek a spouse, Calvin began a search with the help of Bucer and others.

The first candidate was a wealthy woman whose brother was a strong supporter of Calvin. Everyone—except Calvin himself—was in favor of this match. One issue for him was that she didn't speak French. Also, the matter of her relatively large dowry troubled Calvin. Having so much money could prove embarrassing to a pastor who saw his lot in life as one of veritable poverty. How could he preach about the poor without knowing keenly what it meant to be poor, or to be forever in need himself? For that matter, how could he preach about the need to seek God's help in prayer if his own coffers were full? Finally, he feared this woman would eventually reject him as being below her station in life.

Farel then suggested a devout Protestant woman who had never been married. But she was much older than Calvin, and he didn't pursue a relationship with her.

The third candidate seemed more promising. She lived in another city, and their initial conversations went well. She didn't have much money, but she had a sterling reputation. They even set a date, asking Farel to officiate at their wedding. This woman fell in love with Calvin and made it clear how much marrying him meant to her. Perhaps her ardent heart put him off, making him wonder if he could ever respond to her love in kind. Eventually, Calvin took the coward's way out—he asked his brother, Antoine, then living with him, to break up the relationship for him.

Finally, perhaps at Bucer's suggestion, Calvin thought of the young widow of John Storder, a refugee from the Catholic town of Liege in Germany. Among the many who escaped to Strasbourg because of its more open and accepting religious atmosphere, Storder had been a member of the Anabaptist faith. Calvin, however, had converted him to the Reformed Church. He and his wife, a woman "distinguished for her virtue and gravity," had been attending St. Nicholas Church, where Calvin preached. Calvin may even have visited them in their home and come to know them as a family over the two-year period before Storder came down with the plague and died, leaving behind his wife, Idelette de Bure, and their two children.

Calvin buried Storder and visited his widow to bring her comfort. At some point, attracted to her quiet, pious qualities and her delicate beauty, he fell in love with Idelette. As opposed to the other candidates for marriage, she was someone Calvin had come to know and appreciate mostly on his own. It is believed that Farel officiated at their simple August marriage service, and then Calvin took his new wife and the two children into his home.

From most accounts, theirs was a calm and loving marriage. In Idelette, Calvin found the comfortable companion he had not even known he was seeking. She filled a void in his life that he had ignored until then. Critics later would call into question this marriage and the legitimacy of the two stepchildren, because they said that her first marriage was not properly recorded. Anyone, however, who even hinted at impropriety risked drawing down Calvin's considerable wrath. Anyone who wanted to spread rumors about his wife would have to deal with him.

Hardly had the newlyweds and the children settled in when Calvin was called away on church business. At this time, the Holy Roman Emperor Charles V was becoming embroiled in a war with the Turks and was hoping to consolidate his subjects—or so he considered them—into one religion. He wanted to heal the rift with the Catholic Church that Luther had begun and reformers like Bucer and Calvin were continuing to widen. Apparently the emperor hoped that if he could get the factions to wipe away their enmity and come to some agreement on the theological tenets of their faiths, he might be able to unite all of the lands under his purview in Europe, putting him in a stronger position for the coming fight with Islam. Calvin, the author of the popular *Institutes*, was asked to participate.

At the conference, the sides agreed to further talks on the possibility of forging a Christian union. As long as the discussion was focused on the scriptural basis of each side, Calvin was eager to be there. It was at this initial conference that he first met Philipp Melanchthon, Luther's right-hand man. They became friends, and through Melanchthon Calvin found out how highly he was regarded by Luther. Melanchthon eventually dubbed Calvin "The Theologian," largely because of all the work he did behind the scenes at these conferences. Doubtless, the two held conversations about Calvin's reservations about Lutheranism, especially its dependence on civil authority and its lack of ecclesiastical discipline. They differed over their interpretation of the Lord's Supper as well. Apparently, Calvin tried a few times to set up a meeting with Luther so that they could work out their differences, but it never happened. Although the two reformers never met, Calvin and Luther held a high opinion of each other, in spite of their disagreements. Calvin wrote, "God roused Luther and the others, who carried the torch ahead, in order to recover the way of salvation; and by whose service our churches were founded and established."

In 1540 Calvin attended the Catholic/Protestant conference at Hagenau, and the following year he went to Worms, the same place where Luther had traveled in 1521 at the request of the pope to be examined on his rebellious ideas. This legendary confrontation between Luther and Catholic authorities had been retold often. As the story goes, once Luther arrived at the Diet of Worms and realized that the authorities wanted him to recant his ideas, he took twenty-four hours to formulate a response, essentially explaining what he believed without reneging on his new approach to the faith. To the crowd who had gathered to hear what Luther had to say, he declared: "Philosophers, doctors, and writers have endeavored to teach men the way to obtain everlasting life, and they have not succeeded. I will now tell it to you: . . . God has raised one Man from the dead, the Lord Jesus Christ, that He might destroy death, extirpate sin, and shut the gates of hell. This is the work of salvation. . . . Christ has vanquished!"

With Luther's courageous words from many years before firmly in his mind, Calvin prepared his arguments to defend the faith. He wasn't opposed to unity with the Catholic Church as long as superstition, as he saw it, was rooted out and replaced with biblical guidelines on what made for a true church. Central to it all, as Luther had said, was Christ. Known for having written the *Institutes* and for having put Cardinal Sadoleto in his place with his letter, Calvin was one of the hubs around whom many gathered at the conference. He had become a powerful spokesperson for the faith and one of the grand statesmen of the Protestant church.

It's not hard to imagine Calvin at Worms, preparing intensely like a boxer before a big fight, when an unwelcome interruption came in the form of a letter from the people of Geneva, who now wanted him back. Calvin had heard talk of this, but most likely he had tried to put it on the periphery of his mind as he prepared for the great theological battle for union of the churches at the Worms Colloquy.

## RETURN TO GENEVA

Back in Geneva, strategically located between Italy, France, Germany and what was then the Swiss federation, things seemed to be falling apart. Immorality was rampant. People fought in the streets over seemingly insignificant slights. Drunks stumbled through town, bumping into buildings and passing out on street corners and in gutters. Gambling had become popular again. Robbers were afoot. Murders took place. The ministers who took over after Calvin, Farel, and Corault left were neither popular nor particularly competent. After a time, a couple of them simply slipped out of town in the dead of night, not wanting to deal with the rising social anarchy. City officials had put "yes men" in the pulpits—but things weren't going nearly as smoothly as planned.

Meanwhile, the politicians who had masterminded Calvin's banishment fell out of favor. One of them fled the city while three others were condemned to death as "traitors for negotiating the unhappy treaty" that sent Calvin and the others packing. Especially after they'd read Calvin's striking letter to Cardinal Sadoleto, rebuking the cardinal for wanting to bring Catholicism and its attendant problems back to Geneva, the politicians began to rue the day they told Calvin to leave. They realized that in Calvin, that slight but furiously active man, they had a leader who could address the immorality sweeping Geneva and, through his writings and preaching, offer a better, brighter way of living.

At the same time, it's important to note that there was no popular groundswell among the citizens to bring Calvin back. The invitation for Calvin to return came in part because Farel's followers had been quietly working behind the scenes to change minds and, wherever possible, purge the city government of those who had so vehemently opposed Calvin. So it was more of an in-house insurrection. If polled, most residents of Geneva would likely have voted to keep Calvin away. Many of them were happy with the unruly status quo, and must suspected that if Calvin were to return, the "fun" would be over—at least for a time—and people would be asked to toe the line.

Calvin received a letter, the formal request for his return, while he was away at Worms. We can imagine his mixed feelings, even dread, as he read the letter. "To Doctor Calvin, Evangelical Minister," it began. "Our excellent brother and special friend, we commend ourselves to you very affectionately, because we are fully assured that you have no other desire but for the increase and advancement of the glory and honor of God, and of his holy Word. On behalf of our Little, Great and General Councils . . . we pray very affectionately that you will come over to us, and to return to your former post and ministry."

Did the letter drive nails into his heart? Calvin was finally happy, tending the refugee church in Strasbourg and writing and serving as a lawyer of sorts in the larger negotiations to try to unite the church. One wonders if Calvin felt a cold sense of inevitably run down his spine. Once again came the reminder that his life was not his own. Was this the hand of God reaching out to wrest him back to the scene of what he more or less considered a failure? Mixed into all of this, though, must have been some satisfaction to think that they wanted him back in Geneva. Full of doubt and misgiving, he spoke to his friends. They too were divided on whether he should return.

In a letter to Farel, Calvin communicated his reticence. "Whenever I call to mind the wretchedness of my life there, how can it not be but my very soul should shudder at the proposal for my return?" A period of serious doubt ensued. He felt pulled and stretched between the poles of a calm life in Strasbourg and, at the very least, social and spiritual turmoil in Geneva. He prayed and pondered and asked God to reconsider this new posting.

Then Calvin's friend Bucer took him aside, and they talked it over at length. Well aware of how torn Calvin felt, Bucer finally told him that it might be God's will that he return. Perhaps he could return and accomplish what he had first set out to do. Calvin listened to this advice, gulping back his anxiety, no doubt, but knowing that Bucer made sense. Then came a letter from Farel, which more or less sealed the decision. Of this bombastic letter, Calvin wrote: "The thunderbolts which you so strangely hurl at me, for whatever reasons I know not, have filled me with the greatest terror and dismay. You know that I have dreaded this summons, but that I have not been deaf to it. Then why attack me with such violence as almost to disrupt our friendship?"

Directly after Worms, where after three days nothing was accomplished, Calvin returned home for a month, still going back and forth on his future. The next assembly to debate the struggle for unity, pushed forward by the Holy Roman Emperor, was set for January 1541. Calvin decided to attend. The trip to the German city of Ratibon, in the heart of Catholic country, was long and cold, but the Danube had thawed enough to allow them to travel on a large raft for several days toward their destination. En route, Calvin continued to think about the offer in Genva. He had been in contact with authorities there, indicating his reluctant interest. But he was also thinking about the meeting to be held in Ratibon. We can imagine Calvin on that raft being carried along by the slushy Danube, wrapped in fur robes, wanting to be back home with his wife and dreading a return to Geneva. At the same time, he worried that this trip would be a waste of time: he was pessimistic that this assembly would resolve the differences. These huge meetings tended to take forever to coordinate and then, once they began, little of substance was resolved. "But," he wrote in a letter, "I shall follow wherever God leads, who knows best why He has laid this necessity on me." We must keep in mind as well that Calvin continued to suffer from a range of physical ailments—gout and indigestion and terrible headaches. Such a journey, riding down a frigid river in the dead of winter, must have been a trial.

Arriving at the conference, Calvin learned that the plague had struck in Strasbourg. He prayed hard that his wife and stepchildren were not infected. As it turned out they were spared, but the disease took the lives of two young men who had come to live and learn from Calvin, Claude Feray, a Greek scholar and Calvin's assistant, and Feray's pupil, Louis de Richebourg, a Norman nobleman of whom Calvin had grown especially fond. In a letter to the father of de Richebourg, Calvin wrote that the news of the death caused him to be "so utterly unpowered that for many days, I was unfit for nothing but to weep, yet among men I was almost a nonentity."

Meanwhile, the assembly dragged on, seeming to make progress one day, and falling into ruin the next. Finally, the big issue—the Lord's Supper—came up and derailed the entire gathering. In fact Calvin's view of Communion was not so far removed from that of the Catholics; even Luther had said he liked how Calvin had conceived it. But as usual there was an impasse over the issue of the presence of the actual body and blood in the sacrament. Convinced that the matter would never be resolved and that this Diet would end like the others, Calvin got permission from the people in Strasbourg who had sent him to make the long return journey home, where he arrived in June.

Ami Perrin, then a commissioner and a militia leader in Geneva (later to become one of Calvin's fiercest enemies), came to Strasbourg to negotiate with Calvin in person and smooth the way for his return. Calvin's good friend Pierre Viret had already agreed to return to Geneva and take over a church. Farel also wanted Calvin to return to Geneva, but for various reasons Farel himself remained as pastor of the church he had been serving.

Finally Calvin agreed to return to the city he had been forced to leave three years earlier. He and his wife decided that she would stay behind and wrap up their affairs until he sent for her. In September 1541, he set off for Geneva, this time escorted by an official herald on horseback. Arriving earlier than expected, Calvin reentered the city with little fanfare. Almost immediately he presented himself before the city magistrates and explained why he had delayed so long before deciding to return. Then, taking advantage of their goodwill on having him back, he asked them to choose a committee to help him write a constitution for the Genevan church. Although he didn't inform them at the time, Calvin had agreed to come back largely to see if, as Bucer suggested, he could implement the same changes in Geneva as he had at his church in Strasbourg. The notion of a "City of God" had continued to grow in his mind. It shone like a star on the horizon of his life, reminding him that a civil society that followed God's laws and principles could endure, providing for its people and keeping them connected to a life of prayer. Calvin believed this sacred experiment could have a lasting impact.

Lawmakers graciously agreed to establish the committee. In addition they provided Calvin with a house to live in, a fairly decent salary, and twelve measures of wheat and two tubs of wine to help start his new household. The house overlooked the lake and the mountains, and it included a large garden. They also provided their pastor with a black velvet robe to wear as a sign of his office. Pleased with his new situation, Calvin began to have high hopes for the future.

Besides providing the home and other amenities, city officials had also built the preacher a new pulpit, made of wood and fastened to stone pillars, in St. Pierre. Not long after he arrived, Calvin requested that the bell be rung at St. Pierre to gather the people for a weekday service of penitence and recollection. During the service Calvin spoke about the problems facing the world and asked God to be with the congregation in this new chapter of his ministry in Geneva. They prayed, asking for forgiveness and for wisdom. Then the people left, wondering what this new chapter would bring.

The church was packed on the first Sunday Calvin ascended his new pulpit to preach. During the service a few days before, Calvin hadn't said why he left and why he had now returned. We can imagine him looking out over the church on that first Sunday morning, aware of what the people expected from him. Tension filled the air. They wanted him to point his finger, to speak of blame, to let the people realize all that he had gone through since he had been banished. They wanted him to scorch the air with his words and to cry out against the injustice that had driven him out. What actually happened could hardly have been less dramatic.

Since Calvin's sermons were not recorded until 1549, we're not sure which verses of the Bible he read on that day. After the reading of Scripture, the people waited and held their breath. Ignoring any inclination to lash out at the people for how he had been treated, Calvin began preaching around the same verse where he had left off three years before. It was as if no time has passed since that final Sunday when he refused to distribute the Lord's Supper and was sent on his way. In a letter to Farel, Calvin explained how he handled that first Sunday. "After a preface, I took up the exposition where I had left off—by which I indicated that I had interrupted my office of preaching for the time rather than that I had given it up entirely."

Soon Calvin sent for his wife, who arrived in a two-horse carriage provided by officials in Geneva. She brought her daughter with her but apparently left her son in Strasbourg. Located at Number Eleven, Rue Des Chanoines, the home, although small, provided more space than the boarding house in which they had been living in Strasbourg. The city council had lent them some furniture, and Idelette combined that with what she brought from their former home. Quickly she got their home in order and began spending time in the garden overlooking the lake. Pregnant with their first child, she grew vegetables and flowers with which she liked to decorate their home.

From the start, the home itself was crowded, since Calvin's brother, Antoine, and his wife and four small children also lived there. In addition, people began stopping by the house at all hours to talk to the preacher. Often dressed very casually, he would invite people in, listen to their story, and then offer advice.

Within a short time, the Calvin home began to serve as a refuge for people on the run. One such person was Clément Marot, a French lyrical poet whom Calvin had met in Italy. He had been all over Europe, trying to stay ahead of Catholic authorities who opposed his writings. Marot had become expert at putting the psalms in metrical form for singing in church. Catholic authorities at the time, of course, abhorred this liturgical practice. Remember that at this point the only person who spoke during Mass was the priest. Calvin, however, liked what Marot had done so much that he asked the poet to versify twenty-five psalms for use specifically in his church in Geneva. Calvin then helped Marot to get his psalms published in 1543 and contributed a preface.

Meanwhile, Idelette was hard-pressed to find food and drink for all these visitors and family members, since her husband's salary hardly stretched to cover all these added costs. Quiet by nature, she provided stability to the home as well as to her busy husband. Although she stayed in the background when necessary, her presence offered balance to that of her often distant, intellectual husband. Calvin wrote that she was a good companion to him, largely because of her own strong faith, which allowed them to serve God together. He once referred to her as "the faithful assistant of my ministry." They took long walks around the city and stopped to talk with many people along the way. Not all of them were friends. But Calvin did his best to protect his wife from critics, some of whom gossiped incessantly about the fact that she had never been legally married to her first husband. (As Anabaptists, who believed that civil laws had little authority over them, they had held a sacred ceremony but did not sign legal papers.) When faced with outright criticism, Calvin would fling withering epithets at the accusers.

*Chapter 7*

# RETURN TO GENEVA

---

eturning to Geneva, Calvin plunged into an exhausting schedule. Arising at 5 a.m. he would go into his upstairs study and library, where he would pray for a long period, placing himself, as always, before God, and asking God to guide whatever happened that day. After that, he began putting together sermons and dictating letters and revisions of his *Institutes* to a student. In 1542 Calvin published a book on the forms of prayers and church hymns used in the Protestant church and a new Catechism, this one more accessible than the one he had written when he was first in Geneva. He also began his habit of giving what became very popular lectures, often in his church between Sundays. His first lecture was on the Gospel of John, followed by teaching on Corinthians.

In addition, he was helping to create rules and guidelines for a new approach to governing the city. By late September, with the help of the committee appointed when he first returned, Calvin presented his *Ecclesiastic Ordinances*, or laws of discipline, to the magistrates for approval.

Between meetings with city officials and teaching sessions with students, as well as preaching sermons nearly every day, Calvin was burning the candle at both ends. It must have been a relief to return home each evening to talk to Idelette and explain to her the many challenges he continued to face. Likely, he took comfort as well in the swelling of her womb, the baby that was on the way.

Meanwhile, the city itself was growing quickly as refugees from persecution in France began pouring into Geneva. Many ended up at Calvin's church.

Calvin was committed to cleaning up what he considered the sinful ways of Geneva, hoping to turn it into a New Jerusalem as he had done in Strasbourg. Inevitably, he made his share of enemies in the process.

The *Ordinances* called for a body of ministers to rule the church; a consistory of six ministers and twelve elders would oversee the moral life of the city and hold people accountable for their behavior. This disciplinary body met every Thursday and was presided over by a city official. Although the consistory held power over moral life, it would pass crimes such as murder and robbery to civil officials. Deacons would receive and pay money to tend to the needs of the poor, and teachers or doctors would work with children and adults, helping them better understand the faith.

Calvin was never in favor of turning Geneva into a theocracy (the total submission of the state to the church). Rather he was fighting against the reverse, the control of the state over the church. Calvin clearly defined the power of the church and the power of the city. His aim was not separation of the church from the state, but the sharing of tasks.

The issue of the exact responsibilities of each came to the fore in the question of excommunication. Was excommunication—that is, prohibiting people from taking part in Communion—a religious or a civil decision? Calvin defended the first interpretation; city officials wanted to go with the second interpretation. The company of pastors had to wage a long and difficult battle before finally winning their case.

Calvin maintained the basic form of worship he had devised with Bucer in Strasbourg. It favored the intellectual over the emotional or the aesthetic aspects of worship, although congregational singing had an important place in worship. Services included both extemporaneous and formal prayer, as well as an emphasis on the Lord's Supper. Instead of wearing bright vestments, preachers dressed in a sober black gown, the "Genevan gown" still worn in some Reformed churches today.

In addition to preaching and conducting worship services, pastors were required, once they received notice, to visit the sick. Citizens were required to contact a pastor in case of sickness lasting more than three days. The *Ordinances* also covered an array of moral concerns. People were expected to clearly renounce the Catholic Church. Parents were to give their babies biblical names. And everyone was expected to attend worship services. Later, the *Ordinances* prohibited playing cards and dancing. Special gathering places were set aside to replace the taverns; the press was censored.

The *Ordinances* also called on all ministers in the area to meet weekly to discuss the Scriptures. Soon this group, which met on Fridays, also had the task of examining and electing new ministers. These new ministers were to be supervised by one of the seasoned pastors. Every three months the ministers met to critique one another. Those who deviated in some way from the norms of ministerial conduct were disciplined. If the minister continued to show evidence that he was unfit for office, his case was referred to the elders, who would try to put the minister back on the right path. Failing that, the elders could turn the case over to city magistrates for review.

In the midst of working through the *Ordinances* with lawmakers, Calvin had serious personal concerns to attend. In July 1542, the first year he returned to Geneva, Idelette gave birth to a boy whom they named Jacques. The boy died after two weeks, plunging both mother and father into deep grief. In August of that year, Calvin wrote his friend Pierre Viret, the pastor in Lausanne, acknowledging on behalf of his wife Viret's letter of sympathy and prayer: "She would like to answer with her own hand, but she has not even the strength to dictate a few words. The Lord has dealt us a grievous blow, in taking from us our son, but He is our Father and knows what is best for his children." Even here, Calvin's deep faith allowed him to accept the death of his children. Suffering was the human lot, he believed, but it could only serve God's ultimate purposes in our lives if we continued in faith. "Our illnesses surely not only humble us by showing our weakness," he wrote, "but they should also encourage us to examine ourselves so as to acknowledge our weakness and take refuge in God's mercy."

Idelette certainly prayed as well, but she struggled even more. The birth of Jacques sapped her of energy, leaving her with little defense against the tuberculosis she soon contracted. She became pregnant again in 1544, giving birth to a daughter who lived only a few days. This debilitated her even more. She quickly became pregnant a third time, but lost that child as well. The gossips whispered maliciously among themselves that the deaths of these children were punishment from God for Idelette's first marriage, which, they alleged, had no legal basis.

Even through these personal tragedies, Calvin continued his campaign to make Geneva a city of God. In the beginning he was fairly successful. The lawmakers liked him and were pleased that he had returned. They gave him the title "Moderator of the pastors in Geneva." Calvin didn't care much for titles, but being moderator gave him a little more power to institute his changes. Above all, he wanted to find ways to weave the principles of God's kingdom through all aspects of city life, with the church being the dominant force in society. Calvin never ran for political office, nor did he ever hold any city position, but as a trained lawyer he skillfully moved through the city government a range of projects, including a sewer system for this walled city that was bisected by a river and connected by two bridges.

Another of Calvin's accomplishments was to divide Geneva into three parishes. Each parish had a church. Sermons were offered on Sunday, Monday, Wednesday, and Friday. Children gathered on Saturdays at their church to be taught catechism.

Getting the *Ordinances* passed into law took several months, and it wasn't easy. Some people in Geneva didn't like where Calvin was heading. They suspected he was grasping for personal power, pushing his laws through in order to make himself a Protestant pope. This time, according to Beza, Calvin handled the criticism better than he had before: "These difficulties were overcome by the constancy and remarkable moderation of Calvin."

By the end of November, city officials approved the first version of Calvin's *Ordinances*. In January they became law after being passed by the citizens. This was one step in bringing about Calvin's lofty goal of regulating the city according to God's will—a task Calvin never fully accomplished, as his own theology would predict.

Calvin considered the most important section of the *Ordinances* to be the office of elder, charged with the duty "to watch over the life of each individual, to admonish affectionately those who are seen to err and to lead a disorderly life." Elders and others were to keep an eye out for friends and neighbors who were straying from the faith or living in ways not in accordance with the *Ordinances*. When a person refused to change his or her ways, the elders would turn the person over to the consistory.

Calvin often attended the consistory meetings and occasionally presided as vice president. Normally he said very little, preferring to watch and listen. This body could go as far as excommunicating a person, but city officials wanted that power for themselves. A seesaw battle began on this point, with the council constantly changing its mind about who could excommunicate people. Any offence that went beyond excommunication had to be handled by civil authorities. This was agreeable to Calvin, who believed that the state, like the church, had its own responsibilities before God: "the Church has no power of the sword to punish or to coerce, no authority to compel, no prisons, fines or other punishments, like those inflicted by the civil magistrate." Still, the consistory held significant power in the city itself.

In addition to his many other duties, Calvin served as a formal statesman for the city. During his early years in Geneva, this involved representing city officials to broker a peace between the city and Berne. In 1540, just before Calvin returned to Geneva, the city had nearly gone to war with Berne over various issues. Calvin traveled to Basel to work on an agreement. He continued the work throughout 1542 and 1543; finally, in 1544, the two cities signed a treaty and assumed better relations once again.

## FROM THE CONSISTORY'S MINUTES

The consistory came into being in 1542, with twelve lay elders selected annually by the magistrates and a varying number of pastors over the years. It is revealing to examine the range of cases that came before the consistory.

During one evening service, a woman referred to as "The Wife of Laurent Symont" apparently broke out in laughter upon hearing a man behind her talk about people who would kiss relics, even if the relic was simply a normal clock. After hearing her case, the consistory "admonished her to be more steady in the future and not mock the Word of God in this way."

In the case of "Robert, the pack-saddler," a man who apparently had been missing Sunday services had been ordered to be more attentive to his duties. When he failed to appear at one of the Thursday consistory meetings, and then showed up the following week, they asserted their power by peppering him with many questions, most of which he had a hard time answering. They concluded that this man was not taking his faith seriously. According to the records, "The Consistory remanded him to present himself every Thursday from now until Easter, and after Easter until he is fully instructed in the fear of God."

Apparently "Amyed Darnex of Bourdingy, living in Satigny" had never had his six-year-old child formally baptized. Instead he had taken the child to be baptized by a woman named Clauda. The consistory advised "that he be put in prison to learn more from him and that he make a public apology and be admonished." They wanted civil magistrates to make an example of him so others in town would be reminded of the significance of having their children properly baptized.

In the case of "Andriaz, widow of Gonyn Genod," a midwife reportedly invoked the help of the virgin Mary in helping a mother deliver a healthy child. The woman told the consistory that the words "virgin Mary" sometimes slipped from her mouth, and that she was sorry. Weeping, she admitted her mistake and acknowledged that "truly none has the power but God." The consistory admonished her and told her to stop invoking the virgin Mary when helping women give birth.

Other cases involved women caught praying the rosary, muttering in church during the sermon, drunkards, fornicators, and those who "lead dishonest lives." While some criticized the consistory as Calvin's invention for punishment and control of the people of Geneva, Calvin contended that it did not punish people. Rather, he said, it prescribed "medicines to bring sinners back to our Lord."

Calvin's consistory did help turn the city around, making it safe and secure. As a result, businesses located there and the economy began to thrive. In fact, one prominent theme in Calvin's writing is that work and business in general are holy endeavors. Human beings are called by God to work. In Calvin's mind, work was a form of prayer performed and offered to the God who created this world—a partnership in God's own creative work. While money meant little to Calvin and, if anything, had a corrupting influence, he considered work a godly activity.

## UNDER PRESSURE

Calvin remained under tremendous pressure as he sought to thoroughly enact his *Ordinances*. Even his fellow preachers in the early years were often at odds with him—a problem that wasn't resolved until 1544, when he was able to fill the city with foreign-born preachers from France.

When he wasn't struggling with fellow preachers, politicians, and other critics, he had to deal with the impact of plague and famine on the citizens of Geneva. At this time the hospital for plague victims was located outside the walls of the city. City officials wanted a preacher to attend to the spiritual needs of those suffering this often-fatal disease. Beza writes that lots were thrown among three ministers, one of whom was Calvin. The duty fell on Sebastian Castello, who "impudently refused to undertake the burden." Since city officials wouldn't allow lots to be thrown again, despite Calvin's argument that that would be the fairest way to choose someone, a third minister, Peter Blanchest, was given the job. Apparently officials believed that Calvin was too important to the city to risk the danger of succumbing to the plague—and Calvin didn't argue. As ordered, Blanchest went to tend to the plague victims. He walked and prayed among them. He watched them die and helped bury some. In a short time, he too grew ill and died. His death was seen by many as an evil omen—even a man of God could be felled by this disease that seemed to have a life of its own.

Some people in the city worried that Blanchest's death may have been instigated by witches who had made a pact with devil. In an era of modern medicine that treats such diseases with the tools of science and medicine, this idea may sound strange. But in sixteenth-century Europe, as well as America, people believed that the plague was caused by evil forces at work. And in fact there were a few people who maliciously spread the disease, wiping contaminated rags on doorknobs and even on people. These people—though relatively few in number—did not escape Calvin's wrath, or the wrath of city officials. To Calvin and others, they represented the direct work of Satan. Between January of 1545 and March of 1546, more than forty people were arrested and prosecuted as witches for spreading the plague. Under torture, many of them admitted their connection to the endeavor; they spoke of an evil conspiracy overseen by Satan. Some of these people were put to death. Calvin didn't sign their death warrants, but he didn't oppose them either. He saw this punishment as one way to purge the city of Satan's very real influence. Most people believed that without taking a stand to darkness, sin, and pestilence, these evil spirits would only spread.

At the same time witches were being prosecuted and killed, Calvin took on the cause of the Waldensians, many of whom were slaughtered for their anti-Catholic beliefs. This group of believers from Provence in France was staunchly opposed to telling falsehoods or taking oaths for any reason. They also opposed the notion of purgatory, and they believed that the sacraments were valid only if administered by a priest who was in good standing and deemed worthy. Spurred on by the local Catholic cardinals, soldiers swooped in and brutally attacked them. They speared women with spikes and smashed the skulls of babies on stone walls. They burned homes and barns and farm fields. Entire families were stabbed and stomped to death. In all, some 3,600 men, women, and children were slaughtered. Some escaped into the forests and made their way to Switzerland, where they talked about what had happened to them.

Distraught, Calvin brought some of these survivors into his own home and found homes for others. He tracked down food, clothing, and jobs for them. But he didn't stop there. In the span of three weeks he traveled to Berne, Aurich, Schaffhausen, Basel, and Strasbourg to gain support for survivors of the slaughter. Calvin addressed the deputies of the Cantons at the Diet of Arau, pleading for those in attendance to do all they could to care for the survivors.

The Waldensian slaughter deeply disturbed him. Calvin knew them as devout and sincere people who didn't deserve such a bloody fate. To Farel he wrote, "Such was the savage cruelty of the persecutors, that neither young girls, nor pregnant women, nor infants were spared. So great is the atrocious cruelty of this proceeding, that I grow bewildered when I reflect upon it. How, then, shall I express it in words? . . . I write, worn out with sadness, and not without tears, which so burst forth, that every now and then they interrupt my words."

Meanwhile, Castello, the minister who had refused to minister to people with the plague, began to find fault with Calvin on other matters. Castello was a skilled teacher, biblical scholar, and preacher, but he was also a troublemaker. He argued that Calvin was derelict in his reading of the Bible in at least two places—the Song of Solomon and the doctrine of Christ's descent into hell. Calvin denied that Christ actually descended into hell. Instead he believed that this statement describes the agonies of soul begun in the Garden of Gethsemane as Christ suffered God's judgment on sinners. As for the Song of Solomon, Castello argued that it was a human love lament, and a highly sexual one at that, a way that many scholars read it today. Calvin held the traditional view that this passage referred to God's love for his church.

After Castello began making his charges against Calvin and tirelessly pursuing them, Calvin registered a complaint against him. The consistory acted quickly. With little discussion, they told Castello he had to leave Geneva. Angrily he headed for Basel, where he became a professor of Greek, attracting many students and held in high regard by many people in Basel. But this incident made him a lifelong opponent of Calvin's. His hatred for the reformer simmered for many years, over the years breaking out whenever he had the chance to cast aspersions on Calvin.

## CALVIN AND THE LIBERTINES

By 1545, Calvin began to feel hopeful that he had more or less solidified his place in Geneva, in spite of those who still opposed him. Now was the time, he decided, to push forward the part of his *Ordinances* that dealt with chastity. He called on the consistory to punish more severely those who appeared before them on charges of unchastity.

This latest crusade caused some of Geneva's most prosperous families to band together against him. This was going too far, they believed. Sexual laxity was common among the nobility, and they did not appreciate Calvin's sticking his ministerial nose into their (quite literal) affairs. Thoroughly upset at his challenge to their sexual freedom, they organized themselves into a group that began to fight Calvin at nearly every turn. Others who were still attached to Rome in different ways also banded together to fight Calvin, not necessarily over the issue of sexual promiscuity, but with the aim of undermining Calvin's influence and the hope of Geneva one day returning to the Catholic Church. Undeterred by their criticism, Calvin began preaching vociferously against both of these groups, especially the ones he called the "Libertines," and wrote a treatise against them.

As all of this was going on, council records in 1546 recorded that Calvin was also struggling with sickness and a lack of money. The council sent him ten crowns, which Calvin appreciated. He returned the money, however, as soon as he was back on his feet.

Early in 1546, in the wake of his promotion of chastity, Calvin was challenged by a magistrate named Pierre Ameaux, owner of a defunct playing card manufacturing business. Among other things, Ameaux had divorced his wife, deeming her "unworthy," and blamed the ministers for dragging on the proceedings. At a dinner party at his house, Ameaux got drunk and berated fellow lawmakers for being too lenient and too dependent on Calvin, who was "only a Picard, a preacher of false doctrine, and an evil man." Ameaux pranced around the dinner table, blasting Calvin's prudery. Saying he could no longer abide this uppity pastor, he asked the others to band with him against this man who was out to destroy all that was pleasurable to them.

Not everyone at the party was on Ameaux's side. One of them reported to the city council what Ameaux had said, and he was imprisoned. After a lengthy discussion, city officials decided to resolve the incident by having Ameaux kneel in front of Calvin and ask his forgiveness. But here we see Calvin at his most vindictive. Calvin didn't accept the punishment suggested by the officials. Instead he got them to require Ameaux to crawl on his knees through city streets as public humiliation, and to make amends to Calvin in public. Calvin believed he had to take decisive action in a way that caught the attention of the people.

Another prominent enemy of Calvin at this time was Ami Perrin, head of the local militia and the same man who had negotiated for Calvin's return from Strasbourg a few years before. Although he sided with Calvin for a time, he complained when the town began to be flooded with Protestant refugees from France. Eventually Perrin became leader of the Libertine party. He wasn't the only one in his family, however, who caused problems for Calvin. Perrin's haughty and, some said, promiscuous wife never liked Calvin. She let everyone know her opinion that Calvin was too strict and unbending on activities that were simply fun and not, she contended, an offense to God. At one point she and her husband were disciplined for lewd dancing at a party. The civil authorities were about to send them on to the consistory for further punishment, but the Perrins argued that, being of high status (she was descended from nobility), they should be exempt from what they considered supercilious rules and the petty men who made up the consistory.

In another incident involving the Perrins, Calvin complained about Perrin's militiamen wearing breeches that were slashed up the side for an annual parade and target-shooting event. These breeches, Calvin contended, were too tight and showed off too much flesh. Once again, this resulted in charges and counter-charges, and city officials decided to ban the britches. Enraged, Perrin left town to avoid seeing his men clad in the more modest pants. In hopes of mollifying Perrin, Calvin wrote him a letter of explanation: "You yourself know, or at least ought to know, what I am; that at all events, I am one to whom the law of my heavenly Master is so dear that the cause of no man on earth will induce me to flinch from maintaining it with a pure conscience. . . . I did not return to Geneva either for the sake of leisure or gain, nor will it again grieve me to be forced to leave it." Perrin was not swayed. He was convinced that bringing Calvin back to Geneva had been a mistake—he was taking his job too seriously. The city had been looking for calm, but it had not been seeking an angry prophet bent, as Perrin and other saw it, on taking away all of their enjoyment.

# Chapter 8

# WHO'S IN CHARGE?

n 1546, Martin Luther died in Germany. Calvin was unable to travel there to pay his respects to the great "ambassador for Christ" to whom he felt deeply indebted. Calvin saw Luther as a mentor and as a kindred soul; he knew firsthand what Luther had had to contend with over the years as both tried to reform the church they loved. At the same time, Calvin and Luther disagreed on some matters, such as the Lord's Supper, an issue that ended up dividing the Lutheran from the Reformed church. Calvin also felt that Luther had pushed too hard for one state church, and that he was much too hard on other church bodies. And Calvin believed that Luther had become too closed-minded and too consumed with what others thought of him in his final years. He wanted to protect his legacy.

At one point, with Luther's tendency toward self-promotion in mind, Calvin wrote that ministers who served the church needed to be aware of their limitations: "We must always be on our guard, lest we pay too great a deference to men. . . . If this specimen of overbearing tyranny has sprung forth already as the early blossom in the spring-tide of a reviving Church, what must we expect in a short time. . . ." Calvin saw fame as an elusive and yet tempting vice for preachers, who were to work for God's glory and not their own.

In spite of these differences, Calvin often mourned the fact that he never met Luther face to face. He continued to credit Luther for helping to start a revolutionary new way of looking at the theology and practices of the Christian church. By looking back to the early church fathers, Luther was moving in a direction where others, including Calvin, would also move. In the end, it was clear that Calvin deeply respected Luther and was deeply saddened by his death: "I have frequently said that even if [Luther] should call me a devil, I should nonetheless render him the honor of recognizing him as an eminent servant of God."

In the years following Luther's death, the church in Germany faced great internal strife. It seemed to Calvin that Luther's church was breaking apart, largely over the matter of the Lord's Supper. With this in mind, Calvin labored to bring all the sides together and forge peace between them. The resulting "Consensus of Zurich," signed in 1549 and published in 1551, asserted that the ultimate good of the sacraments was in leading people to Christ, and of being "instruments of God's grace . . . sincerely offered to all." In this document, Calvin wrote that in the Lord's Supper "we eat and drink the body and blood of Christ, not, however, by carnal presence of Christ's human nature, which is in heaven."

Although Calvin succeeded in bringing most of the sides together, not everyone was happy with the consensus document. Joachim Westphal of Hamburg fought against it and led a wing of Lutheranism away from the ideas presented by Calvin. Westphal's views prevailed in Germany, essentially causing the rift between the Lutherans and the new Reformed Church under the leadership of Calvin in Geneva. Included in this new religious federation of sorts were churches in Switzerland, the Netherlands, Scotland, France, and, to a lesser extent, churches in Poland and Hungary.

## PLOTTING FACTIONS

In 1547, Madame Perrin's salacious dancing became an issue once again. Flirtatious to a fault, she liked to swirl and sway in her sultry dresses in public. When she was brought before the consistory to answer charges of disturbing the peace by her outrageous dancing, she responded by laughing and calling one member of the consistory a swine. Then, as the consistory struggled with how to deal with her, she stalked out and left town. Her flight only created more anger against Calvin. Resentment grew over what some began to see as a confusing system of justice with two sources of authority: the city's magistrates, which handed out civil sentences, and the consistory, which focused on church matters. The lines between often seemed blurred.

Factions loyal to the Perrins began to form, once again plotting Calvin's removal. In a letter to his friend Viret during this period, Calvin wrote that he saw only more problems ahead and predicted that once again he might have to leave Geneva without really accomplishing what he had set out to do.

With the Madame Perrin incident still fresh, Jacques Gruet, a friend of Madame Perrin's father, decided to make a statement. He left a threatening letter for Calvin in the pulpit: "You and your fellows would do better to shut up. . . . We don't want all these masters. Beware of what I say." Although the letter was unsigned and Gruet had disguised his handwriting, authorities determined that he had written it and placed it in the pulpit. They arrested Gruet and searched his home. There they uncovered a mound of paperwork in Gruet's normal handwriting, much of it containing heretical statements. "If I want to dance, leap, lead a joyful life," he had written, "what business is it of the law?" A former monk who became an atheist, Gruet also asked why Christ didn't take himself down from the cross to spare himself all that agony if he were God. And he wrote, "The world has no beginning and no end."

Under torture, Gruet eventually admitted to leaving the threatening note in the pulpit. He was quickly found guilty and beheaded. Although Calvin had no part in handing down this sentence, he criticized Gruet's writings and made no objection when those writings were publicly burned. Did Gruet's actions constitute a capital offense? Once again, this question must be evaluated in the tenor of times that placed serious doctrinal deviation in the same category as murder. The man was certainly a fanatic. Years after his death, workmen came across more of Gruet's writings under a floorboard, calling the virgin Mary a lecherous woman and Jesus a liar and a fool who deserved all he got, a man who was more in touch with dark forces than those of light.

Following the Gruet incident, Calvin once again found himself at odds with his old enemy Perrin. One day Perrin appeared before city officials to discuss a case against him. At issue was whether Perrin had been performing some underhanded dealings with the French—apparently Perrin had gone to France to see if French troops might be willing to come to Geneva should Charles V, the Holy Roman Emperor, decide to turn his formidable sights on Geneva, as rumors suggested. City officials in Geneva were outraged that Perrin would go behind their backs, especially to try to solicit French military intervention. There was talk of stripping him of the power he held in Geneva and removing him from the seat he held on the council.

When the people in Geneva got wind of this, many grabbed weapons and poured into the chambers to defend Perrin. On his way to the council to take part in the proceedings, Calvin heard all of the commotion. Although he could have turned and gone home, he pushed into the chambers of the council and found himself surrounded by Perrin's supporters. They threatened his life. Some shoved him; others swore at him, blaming him for the possible purge against Perrin. Trying to keep his anger under control, Calvin broke free. In a loud voice he addressed the rabble. Opening his arms wide, Calvin said he had come without a weapon—if they wanted to kill him, let someone step forward to do so. If they were there to shed blood, they should start with him. Everyone knew he meant it. This was not hollow bravery, performed as a show.

This briefly calmed the crowd, and Calvin proceeded further into the chamber. But then fights broke out around him once again. Voices were raised; threats were made. Calvin had a few friends in the room, and eventually they succeeded in quieting the crowd and getting them to sit down. Calvin then addressed the crowd, imploring them to remain peaceful and to let city officials question Perrin and decide if he had done anything wrong. Apparently this speech worked. People began filing out quietly, while a few others stayed.

Upon seeing the kind of support Perrin had among the citizens and the near riot that had occurred, city officials backed off on his dealings in France and agreed to let him remain in town and to retain his council seat. Calvin wasn't pleased, but he left the chambers confident that he would have other opportunities to challenge Perrin.

Underlying this conflict in the council chambers was the perennial question of who really controlled city government. Calvin had calmed the crowd, and some people had truly listened to him. Perhaps he could build on that. Then again, city officials had seen firsthand the spontaneous support for Perrin. If nothing else, it became clear that the factions in Geneva were restless for change.

# THEOLOGICAL STRUGGLES

Along with these struggles for power, Calvin faced issues of a more theological nature. One of these was an emerging confrontation involving the doctrine of predestination. Although Calvin was certainly not the first to write about predestination, his views began drawing the ire of noted scholars across Europe. Some were simply looking for a way to diminish the reformer's influence; others were vehemently opposed to his doctrine. His first real adversary on this issue was Albert Pighius, a Dutch Catholic writer who had been at odds with Luther and Erasmus over their views on free will.

In the early 1540s, Pighius turned his attention to Calvin. Although he violently attacked him in writing and speeches, he never confronted Calvin face to face in a public debate. A skilled writer and thinker, Pighius apparently hoped that the pope would make him a cardinal if he was able to tear apart Calvin's ideas on the topic of free will versus predestination. Pighius's writings debunked what he called the doctrine of "the slavery of the human will," that is, the idea that God has ordained the actions of every person. This, he believed, was the main error of Reformation thinkers. Why would one choose to be moral, Pighius argued, if God had already decided every person's fate? His ideas gained momentum, forcing Calvin to state, once again, his side of the argument. As it turned out, Pighius died in 1542, just as Calvin's rebuttal to his ideas was published. Some say that Pighius actually came around to Calvin's position late in his life, having studied the doctrine so thoroughly.

Other opponents were to come, attacking any and all aspects of Calvin's thought and character. Calvin took on these challenges, at times offering his resignation to city officials, which they refused to accept. Although Calvin caused them almost constant grief, they also respected him and realized that slowly but surely he had been mending the moral fabric of the city.

# THE DEATH OF IDELETTE

In the midst of his fights over doctrine and his worries over the splintering of the Lutherans, Calvin had personal worries as well. Idelette's tuberculosis and other health problems were no better, and the deaths of their three children had debilitated her. His ongoing series of battles with critics must have hurt her as well. As the years in Geneva wore on, they had little time to simply relax and enjoy one another's company. Still, she supported her husband, staying at his side and attending to his needs while keeping their home running.

Eventually, so racked with fever and coughs that she could hardly function, she took to her bed. Calvin sat at her side, even as she insisted that he continue his ministry. Watching her decline, wrote Calvin, made him think about Abraham, the biblical patriarch who suffered for many years with his wife, Sarah, over their lack of ability to have children. Calvin anguished over what life would be like without his beloved Idelette, and yet he was convinced that everything, including death, came under God's domain. He prayed hard for his wife, even as he prepared to accept whatever happened. During this time Calvin had a chance to tell her what she had meant to him in their nine years of marriage.

Three days before she died in April of 1549, Idelette asked her husband to take care of the two children from her previous marriage. She told him she had already in her heart entrusted them to God. Assured by Calvin that he would continue to take responsibility for them, she responded, "I know that you would not neglect that which you know has been entrusted to God." Calvin kept his word to his dying wife, and was a father to Idelette's children for the next fifteen years until his own death.

At one point as she lay dying, Idelette called out, "O glorious resurrection! O God of Abraham and our fathers, in thee have the faithful trusted during so many past ages, and none of them have trusted in vain. I also will hope." Calvin was deeply moved to know that she was putting her faith and hope in God, even as death approached. About 6 p.m. Calvin briefly left her in the company of another minister to attend to some business. When he returned a little after 7 p.m., her condition had declined even further. Apparently aware that death was near, she asked those in the room to pray. As they did, she seemed to gain comfort from listening to the prayers being offered. Just before 8 p.m., she died quietly and calmly.

Only forty years old at the time, Calvin never remarried. Perhaps this had to do with his native shyness and the fact that he missed Idelette, having loved her so deeply. In a letter to his friend Viret a few days after the death, he expressed how painful her passing was for him. He was also grateful, he said, for the friends who rallied around and offered comfort and help. During this time Calvin was afflicted with terrible headaches. He said that if he had not spent so much of his life learning how to subdue and control his emotions, he wasn't sure how he would have fared. "I have been bereaved of the best companion of my life, of one who, had it been so ordered, would not only have been the sharer of my exile and poverty but even of my death. During her life she was the faithful helper of my ministry."

For Calvin, love was in the day-to-day business of living and relating, not in some great gushing of emotion. Idelette was his friend as well as the woman he loved, and his sorrow over her death lasted for years. It also made him more sensitive to others who had lost their spouses. In one letter to a friend who had lost his wife, Calvin wrote, "How severe a wound the death of your most excellent wife has inflicted upon you I know from my own experience. I know how difficult it was for me to master my grief."

## WRANGLING OVER PREDESTINATION

Even as he buried his wife, Calvin faced another opponent over the issue of predestination. Jerome Bolsec was a former Carmelite monk from Paris. Having fled France for Italy, he landed in Geneva and stayed for a time. A man of wide learning, he attended the Thursday sessions at which pastors and the public would discuss theological matters. Overall, he agreed with much of what Calvin taught, but he broke with him over predestination. This doctrine, Bolsec believed, turned God into an evil tyrant, indescribably choosing one person for salvation well before birth while shunting another into a world of darkness and eternal damnation.

For all the opposition it provoked, predestination was not central to Calvin's theology—he only touched on it briefly in his first edition of the *Institutes*. In part, he saw it as a great mystery that was ultimately unexplainable. At the same time, bedeviled by anxiety for much of his life, he also found believing he was one of God's elect a source of great comfort. Despite our sinful nature we can find salvation in God. In this, Calvin believed, there is profound consolation. Salvation is all about God's grace and not about anything humans can do to save themselves. "We shall never be clearly persuaded . . . that our eternal salvation flows from the wellspring of God's free mercy until we come to know his eternal election," he wrote. "How much the ignorance of this principle detracts from God's glory, how much it takes away from true humility, is well known." Augustine and Luther taught this as well. Calvin believed that this teaching of God as the only one who saves was a source of true spiritual comfort.

Predestination was the topic for discussion during one of the weekly congregational meetings in October 1551. These meetings were a kind of Bible study and discussion group, attended mostly by ministers but also by others interested in theological ideas. That day's speaker was Jean de Saint Andre, a minister from the nearby town of Jussy, who talked about the teaching of election and the limits on man's free will. Bolsec was in the audience that day. He listened as long as he could, until, unable to contain himself, Bolsec cried out that this teaching was absurd, and that it turned God into the author of all sin. If God truly loved people, how could he so coldly pick and choose who was to be among the elect and who was not? Bolsec questioned strongly whether this doctrine had any real basis in Scripture.

Since Calvin had been absent at the start of the meeting, Bolsec assumed he would be able let his criticism fly without much recrimination. However, Calvin came in just as Bolsec was speaking. He stood in the back and listened, growing angrier by the minute. When Bolsec finished, Calvin climbed up into the pulpit and launched into an extemporaneous defense. He and Bolsec had argued about this doctrine before, in softer tones, and had come to no agreement. This time Calvin thundered out a response, quoting passages of Scripture and sections from Saint Augustine on the subject. Staring down at the congregation, and especially at

Bolsec, Calvin argued that as this was a doctrine ultimately incapable of being understood, it must simply be accepted. In Calvin's mind, Bolsec was trying to overturn the sanctity of Christ's church. Calvin's words of rebuttal were not those of a demagogue who gloried in the election of a few at the expense of others. Rather he was speaking almost as a mystic, affirming that the ways of God are ultimately unknowable. Scripture, Calvin said, spoke about a God who, in his inscrutable wisdom, was able to choose as he wanted, for purposes not always comprehensible to the human mind. Mere humans could never lift the veil around God. "And let us not be ashamed to be ignorant of something in this matter wherein there is a certain learned ignorance," Calvin wrote in his *Institutes*, and may have uttered that day as well. When he finished, the congregation remained silent. Many people looked embarrassed, says Beza. Then, from out of the hushed crowd, came a city magistrate who arrested Bolsec and took him to jail.

Bolsec's position included significant objections, many of which still resonate today. What proved to be his undoing, however, was his manner of addressing them. By putting Calvin in a corner in this public setting, Calvin had to defend himself and the doctrine in the same public way. Bolsec was tried for sedition and threatened with physical punishment. The reaction of neighboring cities and pastors, who had been asked to weigh in on the matter, was mixed. Bolsec, some thought, had brought up some important points. Only Farel completely backed Calvin. Nonetheless, city officials found they could not go against Calvin and branded Bolsec a heretic. Unable to decide how he should be punished, city officials ordered him to leave town.

Bolsec didn't seem to have learned any lessons about keeping his opinions to himself from this experience. For the rest of his life he was entangled in controversies as he bounced from town to town, even trying unsuccessfully, at one point, to win an appointment as a Reformed pastor in Paris. Eventually Bolsec recanted his beliefs in the Protestant cause and returned to the Catholic Church. He then settled down with a poison pen and wrote a scurrilous biography of Calvin. Vestiges of his charges against Calvin are still floating around today. While Bolsec's biography makes for interesting, if not scandalous, reading, scholars agree that his work rests "largely upon unsubstantiated anonymous oral reports."

# Chapter 9

# SERVETUS:
# A DEFINING MOMENT

---

The clash between Calvin and Michael Servetus has reverberated down through the centuries. Today when people think of Calvin, the issue of Servetus often comes to mind. For some people, Calvin emerged from the fight with Servetus as a dictatorial devil; many others heralded Calvin for his unbending stance in defending the Christian faith. The truth likely can be found somewhere in between these two views.

Servetus was most likely born in the old Spanish kingdom of Aragon around 1509, making him a contemporary of Calvin's. Like Calvin, he was brilliant, and gifted in Latin, Greek, and Hebrew, which he learned under the tutelage of a group of friars. He also read through the entire Bible in its original languages. Like Calvin, he studied law (in his case at the University of Toulouse); later he became secretary to the Holy Roman Emperor's chaplain. In 1531 Servetus wrote a book expounding on his views about the Trinity. He argued that the concept did not come from the Bible. God could not be divided, as he called it, into three persons. Servetus is hailed as one of the first Unitarians, a group that focuses on God as one divine being with Jesus being merely an enlightened human and a moral authority. Servetus promoted this view in his writing.

In addition, Servetus argued that this belief in one God not divided into three persons helped further dialogue with other religions and was much closer to the Jewish and Islamic view of God. Thus it kept doors of communication open, rather than shutting them down.

Curious about the religious landscape across Europe and wanting to spread his ideas, Servetus traveled extensively. Recall that he had made an appointment while in Paris in the mid-1530s to meet Calvin, but he never showed up, although Calvin risked his life by remaining in town to make the meeting. He met and argued with such reformers as Bucer and Capito in Strasbourg. Apparently, Bucer had had enough of Servetus after a fairly short period and made it clear that he was no longer welcome in Strasbourg. So Servetus went on to Basel, where he had been before. Officials there asked him to retract what he had written in his book. Instead he wrote two more books that furthered his reasons why the Trinity was a false doctrine. Born a Catholic, Servetus's views were opposed to the Church of Rome as well. So when leaders of the Spanish Inquisition heard about the debates Servetus was having in Strasbourg and Basel, they ordered his arrest.

Servetus had no intention of facing the Inquisition. He knew that if he were brought before that body, he wouldn't make it out alive. The Inquisition sentenced him to death in absentia about 1533. By that time, Servetus had changed his name to Michael Villenjeuve and moved on to Paris, where he lectured in mathematics and began the study of medicine, in which he excelled. He is said to have anticipated the discovery of the circulation of the blood in the human body, which was credited to William Harvey in the 1600s in England. He also wrote a popular medical text on medicinal syrups.

Still using the name Villenjeuve, he edited a book on geography and wrote one on astrology. The subject of this book—how the stars helped to shape personalities here on earth—got him into trouble with his medical colleagues. He left Paris and ended up in Vienne, where he connected with the archbishop, Pierre Palmier, whom he had met in Paris, and became his personal physician. The archbishop hated Calvin. No doubt he would have been upset if he had known that around this time Servetus, still searching for answers, wrote Calvin a letter to ask a few questions on the divinity of Christ and on the significance of baptism. Apparently Calvin knew that Servetus was going by a different name, but he did not bring that to the attention of the archbishop. At this point Calvin as a rule refused to have any direct dealings with Catholic officials.

Calvin did reply to Servetus, however, and Servetus wrote back, this time contending with some of the points Calvin had made. Calvin replied again, this time accompanied with a copy of his *Institutes*—perhaps hoping that would make his position clear. Instead, Servetus went through the *Institutes* and scribbled his reactions and criticisms in the book itself. Along with the marked-up book, he sent Calvin some of his own writing. At this point Calvin wasn't quite sure what to think, but he suspected he was dealing with someone with an unbalanced mind. In a letter to Farel, Calvin wrote that Servetus was a man who seemed to have "delirious fantasies." He also told Farel that Servetus wanted to come to Geneva to discuss matters further. Calvin had decided he wanted no part of that. He informed Farel that he would not vouch for Servetus's safety. Ominously he wrote, "If he comes, I will never let him depart alive, if I have any authority." These uncharacteristically chilling remarks clearly indicate that Servetus had managed to seriously provoke Calvin in some way. The correspondence between Servetus and Calvin lasted about two years.

While much of this was happening 1553, Calvin was almost daily at odds with city officials over one matter or another. He felt depleted, if not defeated. He feared that after the next election he would have so many enemies in office that he would be forced to leave town. Perhaps he hoped that Servetus would simply fade away, lost in his twisted view of God. But Servetus didn't disappear from the scene. Instead he actually showed up in Geneva, the full ramifications of which Calvin could never have imagined. Some of the blood that flowed would end up on Calvin's hands.

Meanwhile, back in Vienne, some of Servetus's correspondence with Calvin ended up in the hands of the archbishop. There is some controversy over how this happened. Some think Calvin willingly unmasked Servetus before the archbishop, which set in motion events that led to a trial before Catholic officials. Others believe that a friend of Calvin's wheedled some of Servetus's letters from Calvin and sent them on, informing authorities that the physician Villenjeuve was, in fact, the anti-trinitarian heretic Servetus. In any case, someone sent the letters in Servetus's handwriting to the archbishop.

The archbishop ordered Servetus arrested and changed him with heresy. Servetus tried to convince authorities that they had arrested the wrong man, but they didn't believe him and threw him in jail.

Unwilling to face certain death, Servetus may have bribed his way out of jail, convincing the guards to look the other way as he leapt from the roof of the jail to safety. In his absence, Catholic authorities sentenced him to death by fire. In the sixteenth century those who were deemed heretics on both sides of the Christian divide were killed, often consumed by flames to represent the hellfire in which they supposedly belonged. Execution was the recognized way of dealing with most heretics in that era. On all sides, there was an almost pathological desire to defend the truth as seen by the institution of the church. This led to some of the best visionaries of that time being executed on account of their beliefs.

After his escape from jail in Vienne, Servetus wandered for several weeks in southern France, figuring out his next moves. Apparently he came to Geneva because he wanted to rent a boat, hoping eventually to find safety on the other side of the lake in Italy. He made the mistake of slipping into Calvin's church on Sunday to hear him preach. Someone recognized him there and told Calvin. Servetus was immediately arrested. In a letter describing his intentions that day, Calvin wrote: "He at length at an evil hour came to this place, when at my institution one of the syndics (city officials) ordered him to be conducted to prison. For I do not disguise it, that I considered it my duty to put a check so far as I could, upon this most obstinate and ungovernable man, that his contagion might not spread any further."

## THE TRIAL

The trial of Servetus began soon after, providing an opportunity for Calvin's enemies, chiefly Perrin and Berthelier, to portray Calvin in a bad light and lead to his downfall. At the trial, Calvin brought thirty-eight criminal charges against Servetus, who scoffed at these supposedly trumped-up charges during a public debate. Believing that Calvin was a demagogue with a narrow interpretation of the Bible, Servetus defended himself with great eloquence and skill. Calvin's opponents began to sense that they might have a good case on their hands to finally drive Calvin away. If only Servetus could continue to defend himself with such skill and ended up being vindicated, they believed, it could be a final defeat of Calvin.

For a time during the proceedings, Servetus not only defended himself but turned his criticism on Calvin, putting the minister on the defensive and almost making it seem as if Calvin, not Servetus, was accused of heresy. But, as he had done so often before, Calvin rallied and pressed forward. He was able to turn the course of the trial away from discussions about personalities and bring it back to the real subject—Servetus's views on the Trinity. Calvin pushed hard, declaring that Servetus was a pantheist who saw God everywhere and in everything. This ran directly counter to what Calvin, and in fact, the whole church believed. Beza was even harsher in his criticism. He called Servetus "the real enemy of the sacred trinity, or rather of all true deity, and therefore a monster formed from all kinds of the most absurd and impious heresies." Servetus's own "vain confidence," Beza said, led to his downfall.

Servetus didn't dispute much of what Calvin charged. He agreed that his view was indeed pantheistic. God didn't hide himself in some cloud. He was everywhere. According to one Calvin biographer, Servetus claimed that even the benches and the floor in the courtroom "were the substance of God." To this Calvin declared, "Then the devil is God in substance!" Servetus laughed and said, "Do you doubt it?" The idea of the divinity of benches didn't go over too well with authorities, and the discussion began to turn in Calvin's favor.

The trial dragged on as different attorneys and judges were brought in. Perrin and his supporters kept hoping that the longer it went on, the worse it would end up for Calvin. To keep the trial going, Perrin convinced the court to write letters to surrounding Protestant cities—Basel, Berne, and Shaffhausen—as well as to Catholics in Vienne, asking them their opinions of Servetus and his views. Meanwhile, Servetus and his lawyer tried to change the direction, turning away from theological matters and trying to bring up personal matters again. Calvin was getting anxious and pressing for a verdict in the case. But it was out of his hands. He had to wait.

Some biographers and historians have said Calvin was the mastermind behind the trial and that he was totally to blame for what eventually happened to Servetus. Others say that his role was more of a technical advisor, not a prosecutor. At the very least, Calvin played the role of a very involved advisor rather than instigator. He sincerely believed Servetus was a heretic and that he needed pay for his view. And he knew he wasn't alone in his thinking. Servetus, after all, had come to Geneva as a hunted man. The Catholic Inquisition had already issued a death warrant for him years before.

## A CHALLENGE AT THE TABLE

By September 1553, Calvin had to take his attention away from Servetus and focus on a plot by Ami Perrin and Philipert Berthelier. Berthelier was a well-liked official in Geneva and friend of Ami Perrin's. Animosity between Calvin and Berthelier had begun in 1548, when Berthelier came before the consistory to argue against their right to excommunicate people for supposed wrongs. Evidently a man of questionable morals, over the years Berthelier kept applying to the consistory for the right to take the Lord's Supper, and he kept getting turned down.

Sensing that the trial of Servetus wasn't going the way they had hoped, Perrin and Berthelier hatched another scheme to discredit and hopefully drive Calvin out of town. Ever since Berthelier had accosted and verbally assaulted a fellow minister on his way to church, Calvin had made it clear that he would refuse to give him communion—unless Berthelier made a public apology and showed repentance. Having no intention of apologizing, Berthelier wanted to force Calvin into a corner over the issue. Soon word circulated that Berthelier was going to attend worship on the first Sunday in September, one of four times a year that the Lord's Supper was celebrated. By forcing Calvin to refuse him the sacrament, Berthelier hoped to publicly expose Calvin as an insensitive preacher.

That morning Calvin trudged to St. Pierre, full of dread and yet firmly convinced in his mind and heart that he could not give the sacrament to Berthelier, or to Perrin if he showed up. Because both men were so highly revered in Geneva, Calvin was certain that a confrontation would, in fact, cause the civil authorities to banish him. He was sure that the uproar his refusal of communion to Bethelier would cause meant that this could well be his last Sunday in the pulpit. Although excommunication still remained in the hands of city officials, who in this case had ruled against Berthelier, Calvin remained adamant that the church, and only the church, had the right to decide if a person was ready to share the Lord's Supper with other believers.

As he preached that morning on the Acts of the Apostles, Calvin gazed out over the crowd, searching for Berthelier. He might have glimpsed him in the back, hidden in the shadows, but he wasn't sure. Calvin must have felt his heart pounding as he imagined the confrontation. Nonetheless, he preached in a firm voice, moving eventually to a point at which he began speaking about the wickedness of those who took the Lord's Supper too lightly. Of course these remarks were aimed at Bethelier. Not even sure if his enemy was in church that day, Calvin finally descended from the pulpit, walked to the table, and removed the white cloth, revealing the bread and wine. In a loud voice, he cried out: "These hands you may crush; these arms you may lop off; my life you may take; my blood is yours, you may shed it; but you shall never force me to give holy things to the profane, and dishonor the table of my Lord."

At this point, Berthelier, who was there with a crowd of his supporters, rushed the table. One man brandished a sword and warned Calvin that he would be killed if he refused them communion. Calvin bent his body and spread his arms over the elements and challenged the rabble to slice off his hands. He told them he would not dishonor God by giving them access to the Lord's Supper. Voices were raised in protest; some said they ought to cut off his hands. Who was he to judge the state of their hearts? Calvin could smell the hot, stinking breath of the crowd and felt bodies pressing into his. Profaning the Lord's table in this way made Calvin all that more adamant that he was not going to give them access to the bread and wine. Then Perrin appeared. Realizing that the preacher was serious in his determination to deny them access to the table, Perrin and Berthelier ordered the others to forgo communion. This quieted the crowd, and the troublemakers withdrew.

This dramatic scene highlighted what was for Calvin a crucial issue—who was responsible for the proper distribution of the sacrament. Calvin was relieved that in the end, a deadly showdown had been avoided. Later that day as he preached in the second service, he wondered again if Berthelier would attend, fearful that this would be his last time in the pulpit in Geneva. He need not have worried—Berthelier did not appear.

## THE VERDICT

Once that confrontation ended, Calvin turned his attention back to the trial of Servetus. By October, the replies were back from the other cities. They were almost unanimous in their condemnation of Servetus, claiming that he was a heretic and taught blasphemy. Then came the response of the Church in Rome. They demanded that Geneva send Servetus to them to be burned at the stake. The Genevan authorities, however, had no intention of handing Servetus back to Rome.

Servetus was taken by surprise when these letters were read. He had not anticipated that the replies from the other Protestant cities would be so negative on his views and so much in agreement that he deserved to be punished. On October 26, the court declared Servetus guilty. With the previous sentence pronounced by the Inquisition in mind, they sentenced him to be burned to death. On hearing this, Servetus moaned in his cell. He had not expected a death sentence.

He sent for Calvin and bravely apologized for doing or saying anything that might have hurt him. Calvin acknowledged the apology and told Servetus that he could still save himself by recanting his words and accepting orthodox beliefs. When Servetus made it clear to Calvin that he would not do so, the minister started to leave. Then Servetus asked Calvin if he could convince city officials to change their minds and give him an easier death by beheading, fearful that as the fire raged he would renege on his anti-trinitarian beliefs. Calvin agreed to try to convince authorities to behead him instead. But the authorities refused to change their sentence.

The next morning Calvin steered clear of the burning. Farel, however, accompanied Servetus up the hill outside of town. As they walked, Farel asked Servetus if he would now finally accept the doctrine of the Trinity. If he would do so, the sentence could still be reversed. Servetus argued with him for a bit, telling him that he believed what he believed, come what may. Then he was quiet. As they reached the top of the hill, Servetus started to pray. When the executioner started his job, Servetus whispered, "O God, O God!" Farel asked, "Have you nothing else to say?" Servetus replied, "What else might I do, but speak to God!" Then he was lifted onto the pyre and chained to a stake. When the fire was started, Servetus cried: "Jesus, Son of the eternal God, have mercy on me." Because the executioner hadn't made the fire hot enough, it took half an hour for the flames to kill him.

The execution of Servetus was largely accepted by cities around Geneva. But there were critics, among them Berthelier, who called Calvin a murderer. Others did the same, then and in the years to come. Noted eighteenth-century historian Edward Gibbon wrote that he was more deeply scandalized by the execution of Servetus than over all of the deaths caused by the Spanish Inquisition. Calvin, he said, had pushed for the death out of fear that Servetus's ideas would win out. He also claimed that Calvin hated as well as envied Servetus, and that Calvin wanted to hold on to his power at any cost.

# Chapter 10

# AN UNEASY PEACE

---

Not long after the death of Servetus, Genevan authorities voted to finally give the church the power of full excommunication. Calvin seized on this as a major turn in events. He believed that his vision for a City of God might be possible after all. But then, much to Calvin's displeasure, city authorities reconsidered the issue of excommunication and took back the power. He appealed to ministers in other cities, and by 1555 he finally regained—and kept—the power to excommunicate. A key reason for this shift in Calvin's fortunes came from the increasing flow of French refugees into Geneva, some of whom were also rather wealthy and influential. Bringing funds with them, these refugees could pay the price for citizenship and subsequently run for office. It was mainly this group of new citizens who took council seats and began to vote consistently in favor of Calvin's initiatives.

Beginning in 1553, Calvin also found himself deluged with young men who flowed into Geneva to learn about the faith. Busy as he was, he still happily mentored and taught these men, many of whom ended up going to France and elsewhere as "missionaries." He deeply enjoyed this part of his ministry, seeing it as a way in which his teachings could spread through Europe. He also began trying to convince the council to let him begin an official theological school and bring in learned professors from all over Europe. Perhaps he thought he had enough pull on the council at this point to make it happen. But, in part because of rumors of war circulating in the countryside outside Geneva, they declined his request for the time being.

The final defeat for the anti-Calvin forces in Geneva occurred on May 16, 1555. Once again, a commotion in the streets was aimed at Calvin. It began at yet another dinner party hosted by Ami Perrin. As the liquor flowed freely, he and his compatriots talked about the flood of French refugees who had been coming into the town, and how some of them had taken positions of power. At the time, the refugees from France had nearly doubled the population of Geneva. These hard-working French people were squeezing out the old guard, and they were starting to take all the good jobs too. The more Perrin and his friends talked about this, the more upset they became. Fueled by alcohol, they decided to hit the streets with their weapons to harass any French refugees they happened to encounter. For some reason, Perrin decided not to join his fellow militiamen and went home.

Bent on vengeance, the rowdy group roamed the streets. Finding few refugees to beat or kill, they ended their drunken journey outside the house of a man named Jean Baudichon de la Maisonneuve, a Frenchman and Calvin supporter who had been elected to city government. An argument ensued, and some in the crowd began to draw swords. A false rumor circulated that someone had been killed. This was enough to inflame the crowd's emotions and cause more fighting. At some point, one of Calvin's backers was hit by a rock. Although he wasn't badly hurt, the man cried out, demanding revenge. This drew the attention of Henri Aulbert, one of the city's four magistrates, who stepped outside his nearby pharmacy. Carrying a baton, which was an important symbol of his office, Aulbert tried to arrest the rock thrower. This drew a bigger crowd, and the rabble-rousers started to call out for the blood of the French refugees. Arguments raged. Faces grew red as threats flew back and forth.

Hearing the commotion, Perrin and Berthelier appeared on the scene to see what was going on. Seeing Aulbert, the magistrate, in the midst of it all, Perrin stepped up and snatched the baton from him. He also snatched a baton from Pierre Bonna, another magistrate who had come upon the scene. Unwisely embarrassing the magistrates in this way, Perrin led to his own downfall. As the uproar grew in intensity, Perrin dropped the batons and fled, with Berthelier close behind. But the night's activities weren't over yet.

Before tempers could cool, more rumors arose—this time that French refugees had gathered elsewhere in town near a building in which they had been storing weapons and were ready for retaliation. The Perrin party moved as one in that direction. Another confrontation occurred. Again, the violence consisted more of hot words and curses than actual bloodshed. Finally, at around midnight, Genevan police officials arrived. They were able to quiet the crowd and quell the near-riot, and the crowd began drifting home.

By the light of the next day, it was clear that this had been a spur-of-moment outpouring of anger on the part of the Perrin and his followers, rather than a well-conceived plot. But Calvin's supporters didn't care what the reasons were for the trouble. The French refugees quickly lodged complaints about Perrin and his comrades. Many witnesses came before city officials, making a strong case for their fears. On May 24, city officials decided to formally charge and arrest Perrin and his followers. On June 3, Perrin and four others were sentenced to death. By then, though, they had fled. City officials pursued others who had caused trouble in the streets. Two of the so-called rioters were found and executed; others, including their wives, received lesser forms of punishment. The authorities made it clear that anyone who tried to bring Perrin back to Geneva would be killed. And so the era of Perrin's influence finally ended.

## CALVIN IN THE PULPIT

An uneasy peace settled on Geneva. It began to seem possible that Calvin and his followers might triumph in this climate of diminishing opposition. One morning, not long after the conflict in the streets, Calvin took to the pulpit at St. Pierre. He used part of his sermon to defend himself and stave off criticism, addressing the recent events in the city and the changes this shift in government might mean.

We can envision Calvin, clad in a black robe, standing in his beloved pulpit, perhaps the space in which he felt most comfortable. Above him soared the huge vaulted ceiling of the Gothic-style cathedral. Years before, these surroundings had been returned to simplicity—stripped of altars, statues, paintings, and unnecessary furnishings. All that remained of the Catholic past were the stunning stained glass windows. This house of worship, and perhaps even this very pulpit, was in many ways the intellectual core of the Reformation. From here Calvin had delivered thousands of sermons, ringing out words that expressed a deeply personal faith and a vividly real Christ. As on most Sundays, the cathedral was packed with over a thousand people, wanting to hear what Calvin had to say about the troubles in the streets. They knew he would not hold back.

In this setting, Calvin began to speak. "There are those who will complain as soon as one talks of doing justice, that one is bloodthirsty, that there is nothing but cruelty. . . . And not only will the gallow-birds talk so—I speak of those whose sins and crimes are manifest—but their henchmen in the taverns, who imitate the preachers. Oh, they know how to invoke humanity and mercy, and it seems to them that I spare blood no more than they do wine, which they swill and guzzle without measure or judgment. But such blasphemies are addressed to God and not to men."

This excerpt gives us a feel for the white-hot manner of Calvin's preaching. Calvin viewed preaching as the core of his ministry: it was the most effective means of reaching people and accomplishing the reformation of the city. From the pulpit he saw his task primarily as a good communicator. While he was a careful interpreter of Scripture and formulator of doctrines, Calvin believed a sermon was far more than the interpretation of Scripture—it was also an opportunity to apply the Scriptures to people's daily life in the city. Although he normally kept his sermon tightly connected to the biblical text he was preaching from, there were times when he used the pulpit to present broader subjects, as he did that day.

In another sermon, just before a city election, Calvin preached on getting out the vote. He also used the opportunity to give his flock a sense for whom to cast their ballot. He called on them "to think carefully and to take God as our president and governor in our elections, and to make our choice with a pure conscience without regard to anything except the honor and glory of God in the security and defense of the republic." He wasn't telling them to vote for God, but for godly people.

Calvin often preached three times on Sundays. These sermons proved to be so popular that he also started to lecture during the week. Eventually, as more and more competent pastors began working in Geneva, he was able to cut back on his preaching. Beza says that Calvin preached nearly two hundred and ninety sermons a year. He also gave nearly two hundred lectures on the Scriptures. During his entire ministry in Geneva, he preached more than two thousand sermons.

Calvin's usual practice was to preach through the Bible verse by verse, speaking from notes that he written with a quill pen and ink. His sermons averaged about six thousand words in length and usually took him an hour to deliver. In his *Ordinances*, Calvin wrote that that the preacher's job was to "proclaim the Word of God, to instruct, admonish, exhort and censure, both in public and private." In other words, the preacher needed to muster his flock for the service of God.

Calvin's liturgy itself was simple, as described earlier in this book. As a result, the focus of Reformed services was on the sermon, addressed to the everyday trials and challenges of the people. From 1549 on, the church hired someone to transcribe Calvin's sermons. Many of them were also published in book form.

Although being in the pulpit mattered most to Calvin, he did not neglect his other duties as a pastor. Between 1550 and 1559, Calvin performed about two hundred seventy weddings and fifty baptisms. He also visited parishioners in their homes and did what he could to train and mentor a whole new generation of preachers.

In the late 1550s, Calvin preached a sermon on Ephesians, the thirty-eighth one he had given in a series on the letters of Paul. The text was Ephesians 5:18-19: "And do not be drunk with wine, wherein is looseness, but be filled with the Spirit. Talking among yourselves in psalms, praises, and spiritual songs, singing and making melody in your heart to the Lord." He began to preach after reading that verse for the day.

"We have already seen how God is offended when men abuse the benefits which he would have applied to such purpose as he shows by his Word, and therefore all intemperance and drunkenness ought to be shunned by the faith," Calvin began, expounding clearly on the words Saint Paul had written centuries before to the Ephesians. Drunkenness, he said, divided people from God and the nourishment given by Jesus Christ. Getting drunk turns people inward and seals them off from God's grace.

"Now, if instead of being drawn upward, men become so brutish as to lose all reason and manhood, it is an utter perversion of the order of nature, it is like provoking God in his own good gifts. And therefore in order to keep us in sobriety and orderly behavior, St. Paul says, not without cause, that we must keep ourselves from being overcome and vanquished by wine."

Perhaps Calvin was thinking of the drunken night that turned out to be Ami Perrin's downfall when he preached that day. In any case, the subject of this sermon was appropriate for the people of Geneva as, despite all of Calvin's efforts, taverns still filled the streets of Geneva, and people still filled the taverns.

Calvin then hammered home another point: "The thing we have to remember, in effect, from this passage is that all they who gorge themselves in that way and cannot satisfy themselves except by acting like beasts, clearly show that they do not have so much as one drop of faith, or fear of God, or of religion in them."

He went on to talk about the importance of prayer when dealing with the desire to be consumed by wine and other earthly delights. He also touched on the subject of magistrates and others in high stations being given their positions by God, and bearing the responsibility "to bear the pains and cares that belong to their office." Paul was saying, said Calvin, that we are all dependent on one another; we all need to help one another and turn to God to receive the strength of mind and heart to soberly do his will. As such, the magistrates' task was to make and enforce laws that curb licentiousness.

Characteristically Calvin ended his sermon with a plea for his listeners to change their behavior with the help of God. "Now let us fall down before the majesty of our good God, with acknowledgement of our faults, praying to him to make us feel them that it may draw us to true repentance, and make us profit from it day to day." This solid, practical sermon was aimed squarely at people's behavior, with point after point coming straight out of Scripture. Calvin closed with an appeal for repentance and the reception of God's grace and power.

# SPREADING THE FAITH

Throughout the late 1550s, in addition to his other duties, Calvin spent as much time as he could with the young men who arrived in Geneva from France and elsewhere, wanting to learn how to be ministers and preachers of the Word. The foundation of his teaching was how to apply a clear understanding of the Bible in all aspects of ministry. Calvin cautioned these ministers not to form a church until they had created a strong group who would follow the Genevan liturgy and hold the Lord's Supper in high regard. Although his main outward focus remained France, just across the border from Geneva, Calvin began sending his "missionaries" to other cities in Switzerland, Germany, England, France, Poland, Italy, Hungary, and the Netherlands. One of his most famous students, John Knox, took the Reformed faith to Scotland. Calvin labored to keep in touch with many of these men through letters, frequently encouraging them in their endeavors for the Lord. After sending many of these new preachers to spread the faith across Europe, Calvin wrote to a friend: "It is incredible what ardor our friends devote themselves to the spread of the gospel. . . . They besiege my door to obtain a portion of the field to cultivate."

Calvin followed the fate of the ministers closely, hearing about their progress and the formation of many new churches. Some of these missionaries, however, faced persecution. One case in particular caused him great sorrow and served as a cautionary tale of what could happen to these young men who were sent out to spread the gospel.

In 1552, five French ministers who had studied with Calvin were sent to Lyons. Almost as soon as they arrived, the young men were arrested and imprisoned. Upon learning of their arrest, Calvin began corresponding with them. He wrote, "As soon as you were taken, we heard of it, and knew how it had come to pass, we took care that help might be sent you with all speed." Meanwhile, Calvin tried everything in his power to gain their freedom. An impassioned petition asking for clemency went all the way up to the King of France, but the king refused to hear it. Calvin was heartsick when he learned that despite all these efforts, the young men were to be put to death. He wrote the young ministers a letter full of comfort and hard advice. "Now, at this present hour, necessity itself exhorts you more than ever to turn your whole mind heavenward." The five were chained together and burned at the stake in May 1553, about the same time the trial of Servetus was taking up a good portion of Calvin's attention.

# DIPLOMAT AND THEOLOGIAN

After the fall of Perrin and his followers in 1555, Calvin must have hoped for a time of relative freedom from conflicts. But that was not to be. Keep in mind that Calvin's Geneva, even in the best of times, was a walled city only a few bad turns away from attack and dominance by the Holy Roman Emperor and his forces on one hand, and the French on the other. It was a fragile time. Calvin found himself deeply involved in forging the new agreement with Berne in which Geneva essentially won its freedom. He also continued to battle with the ultraorthodox Lutherans over the issue of the Lord's Supper. Through it all, Calvin kept working for peace, often from his bed or couch, laid low by one malady or another. War and violence, he believed, were not the ways in which Jesus wanted his message promoted. "I would always counsel," he wrote, "that arms be laid aside, and that we all perish."

During this time, unwelcome personal issues also intruded. In 1557, Calvin had to take time to appear before city officials with his brother, Antoine, in order to address the issue of adultery by Antoine's wife that had taken place under Calvin's roof. City officials granted the couple a divorce and ordered the adulteress to leave town. It was another reminder of the sinful nature of humankind, and how easy it was, without the powerful force of God's love and intervention, for people to fall into sin. He would later have to deal with a similar situation involving the infidelity of his step-daughter.

Calvin also spent time with Protestants who had fled England under the bloody reign of Mary of Tudor. These refugees were trying to write an English edition of the Bible. Although he wasn't proficient in English, Calvin helped them as much as he could, offering them sections of Scripture that he had worked on and examples of Scripture first translated into the French language by his old friend Olivétan. He also contributed a preface to one of the early editions of the New Testament. He helped the Englishmen put the Bible into measured verses, provided commentary to publish in the margins of the book, and likely played a role in connecting these translators with a Genevan publisher. In both its typeface and style of translation, this Genevan Bible was easier to understand. It was the Bible that William Shakespeare quoted from in his plays, the one that sat in almost every home in pre-colonial America. It became the precursor of the King James Version of the Bible, a text that took much of its inspiration from the Genevan Bible.

Meanwhile, Calvin was also working on what would become his final and definitive edition of the *Institutes* in Latin. This book would eventually be translated into many languages. It became the driving force in bringing the Reformed faith to other countries. As Calvin's "missionaries" went out and distributed copies of the *Institutes*, his fame spread and the Reformed faith made amazing inroads around Europe. In 1559, he got great news that the first Protestant synod had met in Paris and adopted a constitution on Calvin's principals. According to one biographer, "A great national Church, for the first time in Reformation history, was created in a hostile state." Soon after that, seventy-two churches were operating in France.

# Chapter 11

# THE BEGINNING OF WISDOM

Throughout the triumphs and tragedies of his life in Geneva, Calvin dreamed of opening a seminary in Geneva that could provide young men with theological training and ensure the enduring influence of his teachings. He had developed a set of values for theological education: a school whose foundation was the knowledge of God in Scripture, an understanding of human beings as fallen creatures, and the centrality of Jesus Christ in human redemption. Theological training, he believed, should provide a broad general education, based on the ancient writings.

For youth, Calvin brought free elementary education to Geneva. He believed children needed a solid understanding of both God and the humanities. The curriculum included Latin grammar and physical exercise. Students were also required to spend one hour every day singing the psalms. Calvin did not believe in thrashing students to make them learn, and he expected the principal to be gracious, kind, and polite to teachers and students.

Referring to the section in his *Ordinances* that mentioned the education of the people, Calvin once again asked city officials to approve the official formation of an academy. Although they had turned down a similar request before, this time city officials approved the appointment of the first professors, and Calvin recommended a site near his church on which to build. Although money was tight, Calvin managed to raise funds for the school, which was dedicated in June 1559. That school was the precursor to what is today the University of Geneva.

Connected to the academy was a grade school that enrolled 280 students the first year. The academy's enrollment of theology students reached 162 students in its first three years. Soon it grew to 1,600 students. Recommended by Calvin, Theodore Beza, Calvin's first biographer, served as the first rector of the academy. Graduates of this academy included such scholars as Kaspar Olevianus, one of the authors of the Heidelberg Catechism; Thomas Bodley, founder of a library at the University of Oxford; and Florent Chrestien, tutor of Henry IV of France. Wrote one of Calvin's biographers: "The Academy was the crown of Calvin's Genevan work. . . . the final step toward the realization of his ideal of a Christian commonwealth."

Calvin put his large library of books on an upper floor of the academy, along with many of his manuscripts. The words "The fear of the Lord is the beginning of wisdom"—a cornerstone of Calvin's thinking—were inscribed above a portico holding up a large staircase. In keeping with Calvin's own broad education, the academy placed a strong emphasis on the liberal arts. Calvin's hope was to turn out humanist scholars who were familiar with classical literature, proficient in ancient languages to enable them to translate the Bible, and capable of reflecting on their relationship to God.

Such self-awareness, in light of God, was important to Calvin, who was himself a good example of this. Despite his own busyness and unreliable health, he stayed in close touch with his own thoughts and emotions, bending them always to God. Self-reflection for its own sake was useless, perhaps even sinful, but invaluable when done as a way to open doorways to God's grace. Calvin frequently found God lurking even in his deepest doubts. Only by connecting with God even in such moments could he establish the kind of daily, intimate relationship with God that he considered necessary.

That year, perhaps as a kind of reward, city officials invited Calvin to become an official citizen of Geneva, an offer they had made before. Reluctantly, he accepted.

## THE FLESH IS WEAK

Through the deeply satisfying success of the academy, Calvin's health continued to deteriorate. Even when he was so sick that he had a hard time breathing and standing upright, he continued to preach. Other challenges also presented themselves.

In September 1558 he learned that his friend Farel, then sixty-nine, was planning to marry a young lady, the daughter of Farel's housekeeper. Farel asked his old friend Calvin to perform the marriage. Ill with a form of malaria at the time, Calvin replied with a heartfelt no. Troubled as he was by this upcoming wedding, he cut back on his correspondence to Farel. Farel's friends came to Calvin, asking him to plead with Farel to cancel the wedding. This Calvin refused to do, and in the end he told people to leave Farel alone, reminding them of the hard and sometimes dangerous work Farel had done for the Lord. The two reformers remained friends.

No sooner had Calvin's health started to improve than he strained his voice while preaching and broke into a terrible fit of coughing. He coughed so hard and for so long that he broke a blood vessel in one of his lungs and proceeded to vomit blood. From this time on, his health, already delicate, began to decline precipitously.

Still Calvin continued his work. From all accounts, Calvin didn't consider himself above the tasks of an ordinary pastor. He was one of many pastors in town with a job to do. He wore plain clothes and lived in a sparsely furnished home. Once, when city officials offered to pay him some extra money to cover his expenses, he refused to accept it because by then he had not been working full speed and felt he didn't deserve the money. Although considerable sums of money passed through his hands to pass out to needy refugees, he never kept any of it for himself, despite his own scarce circumstances.

Calvin's concern for civic life drove him to write and negotiate with other cities to help maintain peace in Geneva. In 1560 some French refugees, then living in Geneva, began plotting against the French monarchy. Calvin had a hand in avoiding a fight. In addition, he continued to pour himself into training new ministers at the academy just down the street from his home. He helped to compile pamphlets that were printed in Geneva and then given to newly trained ministers to distribute throughout Europe.

Still, Calvin knew he was dying. In a letter to physicians at Montpellier, who had asked if they could help him, Calvin thanked them for their inquiry but doubted they could alleviate his problems. Of the aches and pains that beset him, he wrote, "As soon as I recovered from a [malarial] fever, I was taken with severe and acute pains in my calves, which, after being partly relieved, returned a second and then a third time. At last they turned into a disease of the joints, which spread from my feet to my knees. An ulcer in the haemorrhoid veins long tortured me. . . . Last summer I had an attack of nephritis." He went on to mention several other health problems, making us wonder how this man, now in his fifties, was able to remain so active. A fierce hold on life helped him to keep bouncing back. As he had so many times before, this soldier for God refused to give in to the many obstacles he faced.

But inevitably Calvin's body failed him. Gasping for breath, Calvin preached his final sermons on February 6, 1564. He had to be helped from the pulpit. In the morning he preached on 1 Kings, and in the afternoon he gave his sixty-fifth lecture on Ezekiel, ending with a prayer that mirrored what was on his mind. "Grant, almighty God," he prayed, "since we have already entered in hope upon the threshold of our eternal inheritance . . . grant that we may proceed more and more in the course of thy holy calling until at length we reach the goal and so enjoy the eternal glory of which thou dost afford us a taste in this world by the same Christ our Lord. Amen."

After that, he was carried in a chair or rode by horseback to attend other services and city government meetings.

On March 10, a few ministers visited Calvin at home. He was dressed, sitting at his small desk, resting his head in his hand. He thanked them for all of their support and said he hoped to attend the consistory meeting on March 24. With face grown pale and frail body undermined by sickness, he did make it to the meeting, listening to the proceedings with interest. By this time he wasn't eating his one meal a day of an egg nor drinking his usual glass of wine. The great reformer seemed to be fading before everyone's eyes. And yet, after that consistory meeting, he asked a few people their opinion on some corrections he was making to a new French edition of the New Testament.

# FAITHFUL TO THE END

Laboring always for God, Calvin somehow dragged himself out of bed each day and continued to perform a few of his duties. He gave his last lecture at the academy on March 27. A few days later, on Easter Sunday, Calvin was carried into St. Pierre in a chair. Beza wrote: "He remained during the sermon, and received the sacrament from my hand. He even joined, though with a trembling voice, the congregation in the last hymn: 'Lord now lettest Thou Thy servant depart in peace.' He was carried out with his face lighted with the joy of Christ." This was the last time Calvin was able to worship in his church. From then on, he was in constant pain and in almost constant prayer as his final days approached.

Incredibly, he stayed busy, writing and dictating letters, and telling those who asked him to slow down that he didn't want to be idle when the Lord arrived to finally take him. Finding it increasingly hard to breathe, and with his body pierced with pain, Calvin knew that the end was near. On April 25 he dictated his will to Peter Chenal, a notary in Geneva. He didn't have many possessions to pass on, and not many relatives to pass them on to. The will begins with Calvin giving thanks to God for "taking compassion on me whom he had created, and placed in this world . . . and graciously and kindly borne with me my multiplied transgressions and sins." He then asked God to have mercy on him, a terrible sinner.

The will appointed his brother Antoine as executor. He gave to his brother a silver goblet given him by Madame de Trie and asked Antoine to pass on to his stepchildren at his death whatever was left of the bequest. He asked his brother to give ten golden crowns to Jane, his stepsister. To his nieces, Ann, Susan, and Dorothy, he gave thirty golden crowns each. Still alert to sinful behavior, he dictated, "To my nephew David, as a proof of his light and trifling conduct, I bequeath only twenty-five golden crowns." If anything was left over, it was to be equally divided, assuming all of his debts were paid, between his nieces and nephews, including David "should he, by the favor of God, return to a useful manner of life." In all, his estate wasn't worth much    a total of 225 crowns, in today's currency, certainly not much more than $100. He asked Beza and others to witness this will, which they did.

Then Calvin said he would like to meet with the magistrates and other city officials in their chambers one last time. But they insisted on coming to him. They had to wait for a few minutes until he was ready to meet with them in his room. Calvin raised himself from his bed as they filed in. Once they had gathered around, he asked them to do what they could to maintain Geneva's independence. Even as he lay dying, soldiers in the employ of the Duke of Savoy had their eyes on attacking Geneva.

Calvin then recalled that he had had to deal with "numerous insults" over the years, but this was to be expected "even of the best of characters." He went on to apologize if he had offended any of them as he carried out his God-given duties over the years. He attested to his continuing interest in the welfare of the city and said that he had always acted with the public welfare in mind. Even then Calvin felt he had not done all that he should have: "I again earnestly entreat your pardon for having performed so little either in my private or public capacity, in comparison with what I ought to have done." We can imagine the struggle with which Calvin spoke those words, as he had to gasp for nearly every breath.

A preacher until the end, Calvin reminded the magistrates of the duties with which they were charged. "It is God alone who can give stability to his kingdoms and states," he told them. And since everyone is flawed and prone to vices, Calvin urged them to keep always in the forefront of their minds a sharp awareness of the reality of human nature. People often have good intentions, he said, but left to their own devices tend to act out of self-preservation and self-interest. Only by constant reminders of the laws and principles contained in the Bible could they act properly and for others. People would act with the common good in mind if they were always reminded that God put them here. God by his Holy Spirit would always be present, but people must be constantly taught to have faith in the Lord, and then they would be guided toward righteousness. Tears filled the magistrates' eyes as Calvin spoke. The dying reformer ended this meeting by saying, "Finally, I beseech you to pardon all my infirmities, which I acknowledge and confess before God, and his angels, and in your presence also, my honorable lords."

On April 28, the ministers of the area assembled in his chamber. He asked them to keep working faithfully. "Stand fast, my brethren, after my decease, in the work with what you have begun, and be not discouraged, for the Lord will preserve this church and republic against the threat of enemies." As he spoke, Beza reflected on how frail Calvin looked, how little was left of him. Only his spirit persisted. Yet his words went on, reflecting a bit on his story and what had brought him first to Geneva, why he left and why he came back, and what kept him there. He also reminded them that they, like him, were weak and sinful and in need of God's strength as they ministered in their churches. They would face persecution and perhaps even death at the hands of their enemies. Even so, he reminded them, they needed to be humble, keeping in mind that pride is of Satan. "If your affairs are adverse, and death, therefore, surrounds you on all sides, still trust in him who raises up even the dead." He ended by asking for their forgiveness for the things he had done to hurt them and exhorted them to keep preaching the truth, and to do it with passion, because God's message was truly the only salvation for mankind. He reminded them that the world remained unsettled and that "there are yet among you some wicked and stubborn characters." His final words to them were these: "I return to you my warmest thanks, because during my confinement you have discharged the burden of the duties assigned me."

Then he reached his right hand out to all of those assembled and bid them goodbye. Beza says they all left "with hearts overwhelmed with sorrow and grief, and eyes flowing with tears."

On May 2, Calvin received another visitor, one he had specifically invited. Now seventy-five, Farel traveled to Geneva to pay his respects to the man he had challenged to stay and work in this town so many years before. What they said to one another is not recorded. But the fact that Farel had married a younger woman didn't matter now. The two realized that their friendship and the loyalty both held toward God bound them together in profound ways. In a farewell letter to his friend, the final letter Calvin ever wrote, he said, "Farewell, my best and most faithful brother, and since God is pleased you should survive me in this world, live mindful that our friendship, which, so far as it has been useful to the church of God, will bear fruit for us in heaven."

For three weeks after Farel's visit, Calvin lingered, his mouth moving constantly in prayers uninterrupted now by writing or dictation or conversations with friends and colleagues. His doors remained open, and people came and went quietly, allowing Calvin peace in his waning days. At some point the doors were closed because the visits were becoming an intrusion. He asked that people simply pray for him. Calvin's chest rattled, and he gulped for air as he prayed. It was if now he was in conversation only with God, trying to work through all that had happened to him in the service of his God on earth. Beza wrote that he heard Calvin say, "Thou, Lord, bruisest me, but I am abundantly satisfied, since it is thy hand."

On May 19, the day that the consistory was to meet and then enjoy a meal together to celebrate Pentecost, Calvin asked for the meal to be prepared at his house that day. Gathering his waning strength, he had his bed carried from his room to an adjoining chamber. "I come to see you, my brethren, for the last time, never more to sit down with you at table." He offered a prayer and the meal began. The atmosphere was heavy with sadness as they ate. Before the meal was finished, he asked to be taken back to his room. On the way out, he lifted his head and smiled, saying that the wall that would now separate them would not prevent him from being with them in spirit.

On Saturday, May 27, 1564, Calvin seemed to look stronger and breathed with less difficulty. Beza stayed at his side much of that day. Shortly before 8 p.m., he left. Soon one of the domestic workers in the house called him back. Reentering the room, Beza saw Calvin lying still. The dusk outside was gathering as Beza, realizing that Calvin had finally died, declared, "Thus this splendid light of the reformation was taken from us with the setting sun." Calvin was fifty-four years old. It is said that among Calvin's final words were these: "I have lived amidst extraordinary struggles here; I have been saluted in mockery at night, before my door, by fifty or sixty shots from guns. . . . God has given me the power to write, but I have written nothing in hatred . . . but always I have faithfully attempted what I attempted for the glory of God."

Word spread quickly that night that Calvin had died. People began flocking to his home to view the body, including the English ambassador to the French court. But when some grief-stricken mourners started to grasp at the body and others wailed their woe, Beza and his friends decided to put an end to the commotion. It was clear to them that Calvin would not have wanted this type of turmoil and attention, which bordered on the kind of veneration he had fought against for many years. They decided that they would bury Calvin as soon as possible in the simple manner that he had requested.

Calvin did not want his funeral or his burial spot to become a public display. In his will he had directed that his body "be interred in the usual manner, to wait for the day of blessed resurrection." Following his directions as closely as possible, his friends wrapped his body in a linen cloth and placed it in a simple wooden coffin on Sunday morning. A few quiet prayers were spoken around the casket.

At 2 p.m. that Sunday, his friends took up the casket and carried it to the common graveyard just outside of town. Several people—city officials, professors, ministers, and citizens of the community—joined the procession to the cemetery. But as Calvin had asked, there was no formal burial service. Once his coffin was placed in the ground and covered with dirt, no monument was placed atop the grave, in accordance with his wishes. He did not want his gravesite to draw people who might come to worship his memory and not God. Soon no one remembered exactly where he was buried. Sometime in the nineteenth century, someone carved the initials "JC" into a small stone and laid it in the cemetery, though no one knows the exact spot where Calvin was buried.

In an epitaph of sorts, Beza wrote, "Why in this humble and unnoticed tomb Calvin is laid—the dread of falling Rome, mourned by the good, and by the wicked feared. By all who knew his excellence revered; from whom even virtue's self might virtue learn. . . . Oh, happy turf, enriched with Calvin's worth, more lasting far than marble is thy fame."

Elsewhere Beza wrote of Calvin: "I have been a witness of him for sixteen years and I think that I am fully entitled to say that in this man there was exhibited to all an example of the life and death of a Christian, such as it will not be easy to depreciate, and it will be difficult to imitate."

Looking back at Calvin's life, we can see that everything that Calvin did and wrote and preached had one end in mind: to magnify Jesus Christ

as Lord and Savior of the world. A poem first published in a prayer book
from Strasbourg in 1545 during Calvin's time there expresses the heart of
Calvin's faith. Some have attributed it to Calvin, while others think not,
yet it was certainly approved by him. This poem is still sung in churches
today as the hymn, "I Greet Thee, Who My Sure Redeemer Art."

> I greet thee, who my sure Redeemer art,
> My only trust and Savior of my heart,
> Who pain didst undergo for my poor sake.
> I pray thee from our hearts all cares to take.
>
> Thou art the King of mercy and of grace,
> Reigning omnipotent in every place;
> So come, O King, and our whole being sway;
> Shine on us with the light of thy pure day.
>
> Thou art the life by which alone we live
> And all our substance and our strength receive.
> Sustain us by thy faith and by thy power
> And give us strength in every trying hour.
>
> Our hope is in no other save in thee;
> Our faith is built upon thy promise free.
> Lord, give us peace, and make us calm and sure
> That in thy strength we evermore endure.

*Epilogue*

# CALVIN FOR THE TWENTY-FIRST CENTURY

---

In its March 12, 2009, issue, *Time* magazine named Calvinism as one of the top ten ideas currently sweeping the world. Right up there at number three—along with ideas like having a deeper awareness of the earth's limited resources, the need to stop relying on gas-guzzling cars, and new developments in genetic medicine—is "the New Calvinism."

"Calvinism is back," writes *Time*'s David Van Biema. "John Calvin's 16th century reply to medieval Catholicism's buy-your-way-out-of-purgatory excesses is Evangelicalism's latest success story, complete with an utterly sovereign and micromanaging deity, sinful and puny humanity, and the combination's logical consequence, predestination: the belief that before time's dawn, God decided who he would save (or not), unaffected by any subsequent human action or decision."

Predestination wasn't Calvin's idea, nor was it the centerpiece of his theology—and yet Calvin did teach that the foundation of human salvation is God's grace and justice alone, not human choice or goodness. Collin Hansen, author of the recent book *Young, Restless, Reformed*, wasn't surprised by *Time*'s designation. He spent two years traveling the United States to find out whether young people were indeed embracing a set of ideas that can be traced back in part to Calvin. Along with great diversity, he found common threads that tie Calvinism to North American churches today, especially among some of the youth-oriented emerging churches.

Calvinism is also making a comeback outside typical Reformed circles in non-denominational evangelical and even Southern Baptist churches that are attracted to Calvin's full-fledged understanding of God's sovereignty. Evangelical leaders such as John Piper of Bethlehem Baptist, the Minneapolis mega church, and Albert Mohler, president of Southwestern Baptist Seminary in Louisville, have praised and promoted what they see as Calvin's solidly biblical theology.

"People are surprised when they read Calvin that he was so biblically grounded in speaking to the issues of the day," says Hansen. "He led an incredible life and bequeathed a system of theology and commentary, especially in his sermons, which apply to people of every social stratum. . . . He is a gold mine of biblical writing and thinking." Part of Calvin's allure, says Hansen, was Calvin's outspoken way of expressing his views. "He offered unabashedly the countercultural message of Christianity. He taught what he believed." A writer who was both deft and direct, Calvin could boil down big ideas for people to grasp, not only steering them toward thinking about getting to heaven, but about how to live better in this world that God created and loves. You might disagree with Calvin, says Hansen, but you always knew where he stood. People today, especially the young, appreciate Calvin's non-frilly version of Christianity, with its social conscience and creational grounding.

Elsie McKee, a professor at Princeton Theological Seminary, agrees with the notion that Calvin's thinking is as relevant today as in the sixteenth century—in fact, more relevant today than a century or so ago. There are historical reasons for this. Calvin's *Institutes* have always been read by Reformed theologians. But after his commentaries and other works were published in English a century ago, people outside Reformed circles began to read and discover the significance of Calvin's ideas.

"In many ways," says McKee, "Calvin is actually better understood today than he was in the intervening centuries since his death." People often referred to Calvin and what he said and wrote, but not in the proper context. And when context is ignored, says McKee, the meaning often becomes distorted. That's why it's important to look at the factors that shaped why Calvin wrote what he did, when he did it, and how he did it. Recent scholars have studied Calvin with more historical context, says McKee, "and thus his theology is illuminated by examination of his social world."

One aspect of Calvin's legacy that is often missed is his broad vision for life in God's world—evident in his keen desire not only to get people to the heavenly city of God but to discern how to live for God in the earthly city today. For Calvin, all truth is God's truth, and all of life is inherently religious.

Richard Mouw, president of Fuller Theological Seminary, is a kind of contemporary spokesman for Calvinism. In his blog, Mouw muses about sitting next to a Muslim mufti from Libya for the annual National Prayer Breakfast in Washington D.C. He was asked, as a Calvinist, what he made of the speeches given that day by President Obama and former British Prime Minister Tony Blair.

He reflected on the ways in which both Blair and Obama were reaching out to the world community and asking people to work together for the common good. On the one hand, Calvin would have supported some of the things that were said. "Calvin could use quite positive terms to describe the moral and civic capacities of humanity in general," writes Mouw. "Sin does not destroy our shared social nature, he tells us: 'there exists in all men's minds universal impressions of fair dealing and order. Hence no man is to be found who does not understand that every sort of human organization needs to be regulated by laws, and who does not comprehend the principles of those laws.'" Both Blair and Obama were speaking to this side of humanity, the side that can be swayed by reason and is capable of compassion.

But Calvin might have had some negative reactions as well, says Mouw. Calvin was quick to realize the absolute limitations on any human endeavor. "While people in general do understand the principles of civic awareness, [Calvin] quickly adds that the human mind 'limps and staggers' in pursuit of the good life. In people whose hearts have not been transformed by Christ, civic 'virtues are so sullied that before God they lose all favor,' so that anything in them 'that appears praiseworthy must be considered worthless.'"

Quoting biographer William Bouwsma, Mouw says there were two Calvins—the one with broad humanist sensitivities, the other obsessed with the need for drawing strict boundaries. In today's world, Calvin would support the push toward unity and peace among nations. At the same time, he would be well aware of the limitations on human intentions or actions—whether those of a president or a garbage collector. Calvin taught that leaders always need to look in their own hearts first, for there the kernels of evil reside.

Weighing these two Calvins—the optimistic one and the one who was more pessimistic—Mouw comes down on the side of the Calvin who was more generous in his view of civic and civil activities. Maybe Mouw made this choice because it was a nice day. The breakfast was good. He was in no mood to complain. But he knew that Calvin's shadow lurked in a corner. Mouw points out that, despite all the kind words and uplifting language, the "other Calvin was not completely absent, though. I allowed him to issue his warnings. But this time around, I celebrated the display of civic virtue as I rose with the rest of the crowds in a standing ovation to each of the featured speakers."

Mouw gives a broader sense of Calvin's influence today in his book *Calvinism at the Las Vegas Airport*. In it he calls himself a "Kuyperian Calvinist," referring to the Dutch theologian, pastor, and politician Abraham Kuyper (1870-1920), who ultimately became Prime Minister of the Netherlands. Kuyper also founded a newspaper, one of the finest universities in the Netherlands, and a major political party. Obviously Kuyper had an angle on Calvin beyond the more narrow doctrinal concerns of Van Biema's description of the "new Calvinism."

Kuyper once famously said, "There is not one square inch in the whole domain of our existence over which Christ, who is sovereign over all, does not cry: Mine!" He saw the deep grounding Calvin had in God's creation, and his emphasis on God's continued call to develop his creation as God's *imagebearers*. In one of Kuyper's favorite phrases, he characterized Calvinism as a "world and life view."

Mouw sums up this Kuyperian Calvinism by recalling a phrase from a well-known hymn: "though the wrong seems oft so strong, God is the ruler yet." "This means that those of us who have been saved by sovereign grace have to bear witness to his sovereign rule over all things," says Mouw. "When we go to school or work or play, we are going into his territory. All those square inches belong to him. And our task is to live as people who know the Ruler."

Mouw's emphasis turned me in another direction. I thought of what Richard Muller, a professor of historical theology at Calvin Theological Seminary, had said about the absolute necessity for God. "You find in Calvin," says Muller, "a very strong sense that if God wasn't there, the whole world would be falling apart." God is in charge, and because he is we are able to get along.

Calvin's writing, as well as his activities as a leader in the civic life of Geneva, displays his strong sense of social justice. This concern, which is woven through much of Reformed thought, is akin in many ways to present-day Roman Catholic teachings on social justice. It's this aspect of Calvinism that drives many of the more socially active evangelical churches. "[Calvin] showed a deep concern for society as a whole," says Thomas Davis, professor of religion at the University of Indiana. "He strongly believed that there should be a social safety net so that people could have the basics of life provided for them in a detailed and organized fashion. . . . Calvin brings to us yet today an active sense of the need for Christ to be alive in the community," says Davis. "America can miss the virtue in this."

Though Calvin consented to Servetus's death with a brand of justice we would not tolerate today, we should not assume that Calvin was mean-spirited or narrow in his understanding of the demand to love our neighbor. Showing a wide embrace of humanity as God's imagebearers, Calvin wrote:

> It is the common habit of mankind that the more closely men are bound together by ties of kinship, of acquaintance, or of neighborhood, the more responsibilities for one another they share. This does not offend God; for his providence, as it were, leads us to it. But I say: *we ought to embrace the whole human race without exception in a single feeling of love* (italics mine); here there is to be no distinction between barbarian and Greek, worthy and unworthy, friend and enemy, since all should be contemplated in

God, not in themselves. . . . Whatever the character of the man, we must yet love him because we love God.

Intertwined with Calvin's demand for social justice and equality was his interest in the issues of the law, church, and state. For Calvin, the church and state had distinct—yet not altogether separate—roles to play. There was no strict wall of separation between the two. Rather, church and state should work together while remaining in their own spheres, with Christ always as the mediator. How this would play out in today's society is unclear. Yet there are lessons Calvin teaches us on this front, says John Witte Jr., director of the Center for the Study of Law and Religion at Emory University.

In a 2009 speech at Calvin College, Witte said that for Calvin, "it was the responsibility of the church and state to protect and promote the law and liberty" of people in a community. The church held moral authority and the state held the power of the sword to punish. But each needed to work together. In this we can see the power of Calvinism as it could be used to address the problems of today. Calvin was religious realist, not a theocrat, when it came to relations between the church and state. Knowing that the all-powerful God is sovereign, he recognized that we need not worry overmuch but instead work for everyone's fulfillment and happiness within the boundaries set down by God.

Individual freedom was also important to Calvin, says Witte, as long as people were responsible in their use of their freedom. He called for freedom not just for Protestants but for all "peaceable believers," including Catholics, Jews, Turks, and Muslims and denounced the forced baptisms, inquisitions, crusades, and others forms of religious persecution practiced by either the church or state.

But freedom is only part of a much broader picture for Calvin. Witte highlights Calvin's belief that peace and human rights for all is part of the natural law written by God on the hearts and consciences of all people and "rewritten in the pages of Scripture, and summarized in the Decalogue or Ten Commandments." Calvinism teaches us that the church can be a powerful source for good in society. It is to serve as a moral compass for itself first, but also for the state. The church should serve as the guiding light and even the braking mechanism for the excesses of the state. Calvin's "healthy respect for human sinfulness," says Witte, made him aware of the need to protect institutions of authority from becoming abusive. Thus Calvinists, he says, worked particularly hard "to ensure that the powerful office of the church and state were not converted into instruments of self-gain and self-promotion."

Another surprising voice that has raised awareness of Calvin's lasting legacy today is Pulitzer prize-winning novelist Marilynne Robinson. In her book *The Death of Adam*, she reflects on our indebtedness to Calvin's influence. Pointing us beyond the dour Calvinism of the Puritan pilgrim fathers who influenced so much of the American experiment, she invites us to see its huge positive influence.

Perhaps one of Calvin's greatest contributions, suggests Robinson, was his austere vision of human depravity that teaches us to be chastened and self-distrusting—to doubt, or at least call into question, even our best motives. She notes that the idea of total depravity and the pervasiveness of sin have the strange effect of making us all equals. "'In Adam's Fall, we sinned all' [from the deeply Calvinist McGuffey Readers] expresses the heart of human depravity. But the flip side is that this gives us excellent grounds for forgiveness and self-forgiveness, and is kindlier than any expectation that we might be saints." Calvin did not limit his teaching to the need for self-discipline. He also taught the need for kindness and acceptance, given that these were key attributes of God.

Robinson sees many other aspects of North American culture for which we are indebted to Calvin, "including relatively popular government, the relatively high status of women, the separation of church and state, what remains of universal schooling, and, while it lasted, liberal higher education, education in the 'humanities.'" She notes that in Calvin's very last book, the *Commentary on Genesis*, he writes in a wonderfully expansive way about the place and value of women. Like Adam, Eve was made in the image of God "respecting that glory of God which peculiarly shines forth in human nature, where the mind, the will and all the senses represent the Divine order." When she was created out of Adam's rib, Calvin says "he lost, therefore one of his ribs; but instead of it, a far richer reward was granted him, since he gained a faithful associate of life; for he now saw himself, who had before been imperfect, rendered complete in his wife."

Setri Nyomi, president of the World Alliance of Reformed Churches, adds sanctity of life to the list of benefits that have come to us from Calvin. Calvin viewed every human life as a gift from God, and that life should not be put in jeopardy by taking up arms. In those cases when war was justified, Calvin believed that a nation should sacrifice its own on the field of battle rather than use mercenary soldiers, who were fighting not for a cause, but for money.

Finally, we can apply Calvin's wisdom even to the most pressing issue of today, what some have called the Great Recession of 2009. Although Calvin wasn't opposed to making money, he tended to distrust it. He was strongly in favor of a decent wage for a good day's work. He supported banks and the lending of money but preached loudly against charging anyone a high interest rate for a loan. For Calvin money was simply a means to an end of living a decent earthly life and helping others less fortunate. He would certainly be opposed to the greed and manipulation that has brought about the present crisis in capitalism.

Calvin himself, notes Nyomi, was a refugee from France and in need of refuge, which he found in Geneva. He never forgot that experience, making sure his church remained open to the refugees who fled to Geneva from other countries, and remaining always aware of the needs of others.

Chiefly, though, Nyomi appreciates Calvin's promotion of unity within God's church. In 2010, the World Alliance of Reformed Churches will merge with the Reformed Ecumenical Council—in the process creating one organizations that represents some 75 million Reformed Christians from nearly every country of the world. Calvin would have loved this aspect of his legacy, says Nyomi. "Calvin taught the importance of Christians being united, and I think that is more crucial today than ever before. Calvin was the one who tried to reach out to others Christians of his day."

The reformer from Geneva is still doing just that in the twenty-first century. His legacy lives on, always moving forward, forever seeking unity and oneness in the Lord Jesus Christ.

# BIBLIOGRAPHY

*Author's note:* As this is not a scholarly work, I am listing the main books and other sources, but no specific citations, that I found helpful in capturing a short profile of John Calvin.

Barth, Karl. *The Theology of John Calvin.* Geoffrey W. Bromiley, trans. Grand Rapids, Mich.: Wm B. Eerdmans, 1995.

Borger, Joyce. Calvin research folder for Calvin Institute of Christian Worship, 2008.

Bouwsma, William. *John Calvin: A Sixteenth Century Portrait.* Oxford: Oxford University Press, 1988.

Cottret, Bernard. *Calvin: A Biography.* Grand Rapids, Mich.: Wm. B. Eerdmans Publishing, 2000.

Elwood, Christopher. *Calvin for Armchair Theologians.* Louisville: Westminster John Knox Press, 2002.

Ganoczys, Alexandre. *The Young Calvin.* Louisville: Westminster Press, 1987.

Hansen, Collin. *Young, Restless, Reformed.* Wheaton, Ill.: Crossway Books, 2008.

Hyma, Albert. *The Life of John Calvin.* Grand Rapids, Mich.: Wm. B. Eeerdmans, 1943.

Lawson, Steven J. *The Expository Genius of John Calvin*. Lake Mary, Fla.: Ligonier Ministries, Reformation Trust Publications, 2007.

Linder, William. *John Calvin*. Grand Rapids, Mich.: Bethany House Publishers, 1998.

McPherson, Joyce. *The River of Grace: The Story of John Calvin*. Lebanon, Tenn.: Greenleaf Press, 1998.

Meeter, H. Henry. *The Basic Ideas of Calvinism*. Grand Rapids, Mich.: Baker Books, 1997.

_____. "The Life of John Calvin." Calvin College, 1957.

Mouw, Richard. *Calvinism in the Las Vegas Airport*. Grand Rapids, Mich.: Zondervan, 2004.

Norton-Taylor, Duncan. *God's Man: A Novel on the Life of John Calvin*. Grand Rapids, Mich.: Baker Book House, 1979.

Parker, T.H.L. *John Calvin: A Biography*. Louisville: Westminster John Knox Press, 1975.

_____. *Portrait of John Calvin*. Louisville: Wesminster Press, 1954.

Reymond, Robert L. *John Calvin: His Life & Influence*. Fearn, Scotland: Christian Focus Publications, 2004.

Robinson, Marilynne. *The Death of Adam: Essays on Modern Thought*. New York: Mariner Books, 2000.

Selderhuis, Herman J. *John Calvin: A Pilgrim's Life*. Downers Grove, Ill., InterVarsity Press, 2009.

Stepanek, Sally. *World Leaders Past & Present: John Calvin*. New York: Chelsea House, 1987.

Thornton, John F. and Susan B. Carenne, ed. *John Calvin: Steward of God's Covenant: Selected Writings*. New York: Vintage Spiritual Classics, 2006.

*Tracts & Treatises on the Reformation of the Church, by John Calvin, with a short life of Calvin by Theodore Beza.* Grand Rapids, Mich.: Wm. B. Eerdmans, 1958.

Van Halsema, Thea B. *This Was John Calvin.* Grand Rapids, Mich.: I.D.E.A. Ministries, 1959.

Vowell, Sarah. *The Wordy Shipmates.* New York: Riverhead Books, 2008.

Walker, Williston. *John Calvin: The Organizer of Reformed Protestantism.* New York: G.P. Putnam's Sons, 2004.

Witte, John Jr. "Separation of Church and State, Calvin Style: A 500th Anniversary Celebration." Calvin College January Series, 2009.